Peace in Vietnam

. . . for the world, which seems
To lie before us like a land of dreams,
So various, so beautiful, so new,
Hath really neither joy, nor love, nor light,
Nor certitude, nor peace, nor help for pain;
And we are here as on a darkling plain
Swept with confused alarms of struggle and flight,
Where ignorant armies clash by night.

—*Dover Beach,* Matthew Arnold

Peace in Vietnam

A NEW APPROACH IN SOUTHEAST ASIA

*A Report Prepared for the
American Friends Service Committee*

 HILL AND WANG • NEW YORK

Contents

Preface

The United States is locked in a military struggle in Vietnam which increases in extent and virulence day by day. How did we get into this situation? How can we get out?

The American Friends Service Committee first publicly expressed its concern over Vietnam in 1954, at the time of Dienbienphu and the Geneva Conference. A statement was issued at that time warning against United States military involvement in these terms:

The American Friends Service Committee is profoundly disturbed with the pressures for United States military intervention in Indo-China. On the basis of long Quaker experience in international service we are convinced that nothing but disaster lies down this road. The destructiveness of modern war can produce nothing but hatred, even among those on whose behalf the fighting ostensibly is undertaken, and hatred is no foundation upon which freedom and democracy can be built.

We urge our fellow citizens to remember that a real victory for freedom in Indo-China, as elsewhere, depends upon winning the minds and hearts of the Indo-Chinese. This requires that America first understand that the legitimate yearnings of Asian peoples are for independence and for a better standard of life. These are the fundamental issues in the present raging Indo-Chinese revolution and they are not issues that can be met by military threats.

In December 1964 the American Friends Service Committee

sent copies of the article "Vietnam: The Fourth Course," reprinted from the *Bulletin of the Atomic Scientists*, to over one thousand influential persons, including President Lyndon B. Johnson. This article pointed to the remarkable degree of cooperation between hostile nations in planning international development of the Mekong River Valley under the auspices of the United Nations Economic Commission for Asia and the Far East. The author suggested that this experience might help provide a constructive and positive basis for seeking negotiation and neutralization of the area. Responses from the State Department and the White House emphasized that the "Fourth Course," however attractive, was not a viable option until the political and military situation was more secure. On April 7, 1965, President Johnson announced United States support for enlarged Mekong River development and for regional economic cooperation in Southeast Asia, but the escalation of military activity in Vietnam continued.

In October 1965 the American Friends Service Committee issued "An Appeal for the People of Vietnam," which called upon all parties to stop the fighting and enter into negotiations. Copies were sent to the United States government, to the government of the Democratic Republic of Vietnam in Hanoi, to the government of the Republic of Vietnam in Saigon, and to the National Liberation Front. The statement also said that this Quaker organization intended to try to aid the victims of war in both North and South Vietnam. The statement stressed that humanitarian activity could not absolve Americans from facing "the awful fact of the United States involvement in war and of what this is doing to the moral fibre of this nation." Finally the statement urged that the United States "revise its policies in Southeast Asia so as not to rely on military force."

The Board of Directors of the American Friends Service Committee appointed a working party to study in depth the complex problems of ending reliance on military force. The authors brought together for this purpose have undertaken to prepare a document that would speak to the political realities. Certain ethical and religious assumptions are implicit though not emphasized. It is assumed, for example, that questions of international relations and world strife should be considered in terms of ethical and human values as well as in terms of economic and political power. In nation-to-nation relations men should give humanity itself highest rating in their scale of values. National interest in our interdependent world should be construed in broad terms. Americans cannot disregard the people of Vietnam in the name of some ideological or world-political aim. The interrelationship of ends and means is always important; it becomes crucial if the goal of a free, independent South Vietnam can be achieved only through widespread destruction in South Vietnam.

With these assumptions and principles in the background, the essay deals first with a diagnosis of the current situation. The perspectives of the Vietnamese people are contrasted with the American view. The price of victory through military escalation is measured in human terms. The need to explore how the American people became entangled in Vietnam leads to an analysis of the underlying movements of nationalism and socioeconomic change in Southeast Asia, which have been inadequately understood and often misrepresented in American newspapers and magazines. A section on China recapitulates points made in a prior study for the American Friends Service Committee[1] and applies them to the Vietnam struggle. This introduces the story of the twenty years of accumulating mistakes in American policy in Vietnam.

To the question, "Why belabor the past mistakes, when it is the present that we have to deal with?" the answer comes clearly that the present United States policy is encumbered with misconceptions of the past. The false premises that guide American thinking make a constructive resolution of the conflict difficult. Threading their way through the tangle of negotiation attempts and the stated positions of the contending parties, the authors suggest proposals for a settlement in which the welfare of the Vietnamese people takes top priority.

Throughout the study, undertaken during the period from November 6, 1965, to January 20, 1966, we have been alert to each day's headlines. In such a rapidly moving situation, it is impossible to be completely up-to-date, yet we believe the basic analysis and general line of solution will be relevant for some time to come.

[1] *A New China Policy: Some Quaker Proposals* (New Haven: Yale University Press, 1965).

We have not tried to document the many points made. These can be verified in the extensive literature on Vietnam, some of which is listed in the bibliography. In certain sections in which we are largely dependent on newspapers and magazines, we have inserted footnotes so that the reader can corroborate points.

Members of the working party came to the task from differing backgrounds, but with a common concern for the people of Vietnam and a common anxiety over the American involvement. Two of the group are businessmen, three come from universities, and three are in organizational work in international relations. Two members were in South Vietnam in the summer of 1965; two have lived in China; one has spent extended periods of time in Southeast Asia. Further data on the writers is given in Appendix IV. From varied exposures and viewpoints we have come to a high degree of unity in our analysis of problems and in our policy recommendations. We hope that the writing will convey the persuasiveness of an eleventh-hour appeal for sanity.

> BRONSON P. CLARK, Convener
> WOODRUFF J. EMLEN
> DOROTHY HUTCHINSON
> GEORGE McT. KAHIN
> JONATHAN MIRSKY
> A. J. MUSTE
> W. ALLYN RICKETT
> CLARENCE H. YARROW

Minutes of the Board of Directors, January 5, 1966:

The Board of the American Friends Service Committee, mindful that it does not speak for all Friends, endorses the general point of view embodied in this report. It approves the publication of this study as a contribution to the dialogue now under way on the war in Vietnam.

> GILBERT F. WHITE, Chairman
> Board of Directors
> American Friends Service Committee

Peace in Vietnam

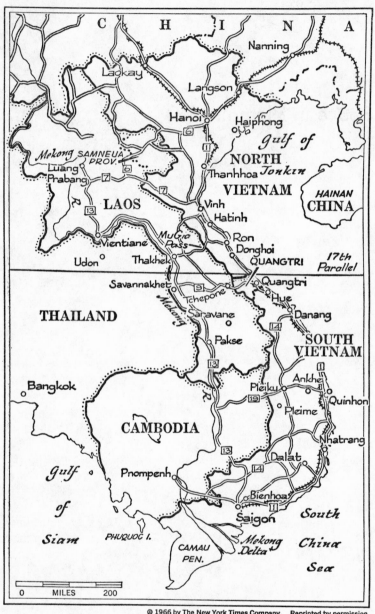

1: Vietnam—Current Perspectives

The scene was a small square in the city of Hué, South Vietnam, on a summer day in 1965. The place was known as a rendezvous for American GI's and Vietnamese girls. A couple of military police were on duty to keep order. On this day one of them had supplied himself with some candy for the children who played in the square and crowded around the Americans. As he started his distribution in a friendly mood, a swarm of youngsters, jumping and reaching, pressed about him. With a laugh he tossed the candy out on the cobblestones. Immediately the children descended like locusts, each intent on grabbing a piece. A young Vietnamese school teacher happened by at this moment, and seeing the scrambling children, he spoke to them in stern and emphatic tones. He told them to pick up the candy and give it back to the American. After some hesitation they sheepishly complied. Then, facing the soldier and speaking in measured English with a tone of suppressed anger and scorn, he said: "You Americans don't understand. You are making beggars of our children, prostitutes of our women, and Communists of our men!"

This incident reflects a widespread attitude of the Vietnamese people when confronted by the efforts of Americans to help them. The emotions revealed indicate something of the impact of American involvement in Vietnam, a physical and cultural impact that has caused grave disruption in the social patterns of the country. In the uproar over Vietnam this reality has been largely over-

1

looked, yet it is one Americans must assess. The attitude of the people themselves has a great influence on our chance of contributing anything constructive to the development of an independent South Vietnam—the stated reason for the United States' military presence in the affairs of that sorely afflicted land.

Americans, on their side, look at Vietnam in terms of preoccupation with the postwar expansion of Communism, which they think can be stopped only by American military power. We are repeatedly told that our strength requires us to become the champion of the "free," charged with the responsibility of holding back the "tides of darkness" represented by the aggressive forces of an international political ideology. This is our rationale for being in Vietnam: Southeast Asia is threatened by Communist China, operating through its instruments in Hanoi; and the United States is determined to stand by its commitment to the anti-Communist patriots of South Vietnam in their defense of freedom against aggression from the North.

This analysis, so easily accepted by Americans, finds little acceptance elsewhere in the world and especially in Vietnam, where the perspective has been shaped by a set of historical factors that Americans do not usually consider. The first such factor is that the Vietnamese people, both North and South, are caught up in a profound social revolution. As is true for much of Asia, people are reaching toward a day when men will be free from the burdens of exploitation, poverty, and disease, which they have endured through the ages. To many peasants, who constitute at least 80 per cent of the population of Vietnam, the national hero and the champion of this revolution is Ho Chi Minh. Although he is resented by others who associate him with repressive land reforms in North Vietnam, he is still widely regarded as the George Washington of Vietnam, the father of his country, the man who fought Japanese occupation of Vietnam in World War II and then liberated it from French domination in 1954.

The second factor of the Vietnamese perspective is the hatred of the regime of Premier Ngo Dinh Diem, who was installed and supported by the United States. Americans have little knowledge of the impact of the Diem government on the people of South Vietnam. Resentment against its repressive measures was so strong and widespread in rural areas that it became an important factor in driving thousands of villagers to engage in open rebellion. Although Americans would like to forget the Diem chapter of history, it must be taken into consideration if we are to understand the perspective of the Vietnamese people toward the tragedy that now engulfs us all.

For years past, village affairs had been handled by local officials known to the people. A degree of basic democracy was present at this local level that existed nowhere else in Vietnam. Early in the Diem regime, however, those officials were replaced by Diem-appointed men brought in from the outside as instruments of control. These officials were all too often harsh, venal, and exploitative. Because they were the villagers' primary contact with the central government, Saigon came to be regarded as the enemy, especially after the Diem government rejected the Vietminh's *de facto* land reform in favor of a program requiring retroactive compensation for the former landlords. The succession of Saigon governments in the last few years has not improved the situation materially, and the resentment continues unabated.

The third factor shaping the Vietnamese perspective is the general feeling of war-weariness on the part of the people throughout South Vietnam. Horror and devastation are inflicted by all the fighting elements—American; South Vietnamese; and National Liberation Front, or Vietcong.[1] A common reaction of the people is to wish that the war would end no matter who wins. The total nature of the destruction wrought in one particular place has been vividly described by a French Catholic priest in an interview reported by Jean Larteguy in *Paris Match,* October 2, 1965:

Today nothing remains of all that region. All is razed. As for the poor mountain people whose villages and rice granaries have been destroyed, they can live only as wild boars in the forest. Before the bombardment, the loud speakers, in the planes above them, told them not to go into the fields and to stay in their huts. They stayed in their huts and the huts were bombarded anyway. Or again the Viet Cong

[1] National Liberation Front is the name which the forces opposing the Saigon government assumed in 1960. They have been better known in the West by the pejorative term, Vietnamese Communists or "Vietcong," a name given them by the Diem regime.

obliged them to come out and machine-gunned them in the fields. Some villages were warned, others not. I have seen my faithful burned up in napalm. I have seen the bodies of women and children blown to bits. I have seen all my villages razed. By God, it's not possible. (*C'est pas Dieu possible.*) Suddenly the priest burst into tears. His nerves had given way. He cursed the war and its attendant horrors and absurdities. He railed at the Americans in English, as if they were there to hear him. . . .

These perspectives help explain why the "defense of freedom" in South Vietnam has encountered grave difficulties. These perspectives also explain the fervor of our adversary. One great surprise to Americans is the fighting ability, tenacity, and high morale of peasant armies from underdeveloped and backward countries, even when subjected to the kind of modern warfare that the United States is currently waging in Vietnam. With our complex industrial technology and affluent society, we find it difficult to understand how people living at a low level of subsistence can hold out so long against the assaults of our various weapons without indications of weakening. Yet those South Vietnamese who have taken up arms in rebellion have demonstrated that they are prepared to spend endless years in jungles and swamps of their country, enduring hardships, rather than surrender. Vietcong fighters are willing to persist, even when confronted with incessant bombings and attacks from helicopters and fighter planes. This fervor affects only a minority, but it exerts a powerful influence over the larger population and constitutes the principal problem with which those substantial numbers of South Vietnamese who support the Saigon government must contend.

In North Vietnam the fervor of resistance is much more widespread, because the attack is more clearly from a foreign power. Western journalists there have observed that the people have now come to the reluctant conclusion that they may have to sacrifice their principal cities to American bombers. They have already evacuated large numbers of women and children and await the day when American military and political leaders decide to level the cities. Factories have been divided into small units, which are being moved into excavations in the hills. Like other American bombing actions in North Vietnam, it seems clear that the bombing of Haiphong and Hanoi will not persuade the North Vietnamese to negotiate a settlement dictated by the United States government. It is more likely to stiffen their determination to resist.

This is the background which explains the failure of escalation policies to bring a quick end to the war. Despite frequent assurances by American leaders that one more step would bring success, we have been driven to ever greater military commitment in Vietnam, and the end of the war has moved further and further into the future. According to Secretary of Defense Robert McNamara, this commitment had by November 1965 brought a total of 165,700 United States military personnel to South Vietnam. According to the same authority, the South Vietnamese government had about 500,000 men in its armed forces. Besides the United States and South Vietnamese forces, there were 1,300 Australians, 300 New Zealand artillery troops, and a South Korean division of 14,000 in South Vietnam—a total of 685,000 troops. It is worth noting that, as of November 1965, the figures show twice as many American personnel in Vietnam as there were French at the height of the French colonial war effort. In 1954 the French-directed army that suffered the reverse of Dienbienphu numbered around 80,000 Frenchmen, in a total force of 520,000, most of whom were Vietnamese.

The size of the opposing force was estimated by the Pentagon to be about 165,000 in September 1965. Just how many of this force are southerners and how many are from the North is not definitely known, but it is generally accepted by United States government spokesmen that even though most of the leaders have been trained in the North, the great majority are southerners. Corroboration of this can be found in the White Paper issued by the United States Department of State in February 1965. The document estimates the total of Vietcong forces as 95,000 to 115,000 at the end of 1964. Of these, approximately 35,000 are said to be "hard-core forces," most of whom have infiltrated from the North; the rest, 60,000 to 80,000, are "local forces." The paper does not make clear that most of the hard-core infiltrators are southern in origin—persons who went north at the time of partition or more recently—but this is admitted indirectly by the statement: "Increasingly the forces sent into the South are native

North Vietnamese who have never seen South Vietnam." The
White Paper, which was intended to document the aggression of
North Vietnam, also attempted to prove that Hanoi has been a
major source of military equipment for the Vietcong. The facts
presented in the paper reveal, however, that the amount of equipment coming from the North and from Communist countries up
to that time, namely the end of 1964, was insignificant compared
with the amount of American equipment captured, stolen, or
bought in South Vietnam.

One of the major justifications for the American bombardment
of North Vietnam, which started on February 7, 1965, was that
it would prevent or hamper infiltration of men and materiel from
the North. Clearly this was a miscalculation. In November 1965
the Pentagon's own reports indicated that this infiltration had
greatly increased since the time of the White Paper. Reports of
parts of regular North Vietnamese army regiments appearing in
the South came in the news with increasing frequency. Estimates
were made and retracted in confusing succession, but the highest
estimate of North Vietnamese regulars was 14,000, as compared
with 165,700 American troops. At the end of 1965, the main part
of the well-trained regular army in North Vietnam numbering
between 225,000 and 250,000 men had not as yet been engaged.
In an interview on November 29, 1965,[2] Secretary of Defense
McNamara declared that recent events revealed " a clear decision
by Hanoi to both escalate the level of infiltration and raise the
level of conflict." He was, he said, "sure that decision must be
countered by an increase in the forces opposing the Vietcong."
The Secretary referred to a statement made by President Johnson
on July 28, 1965, to the effect that the United States would send
whatever troops were needed in the war. He left reporters with
the impression that United States troops would soon be increased
to 200,000 and that air attacks on the Vietcong supply routes
running from North Vietnam through Laos would be intensified.
At the same time authoritative sources in Vietnam reported that
the United States military men there were demanding much higher
escalation and talking in terms of a war which would last five, ten,
or twenty years.

[2] *New York Herald Tribune,* November 30, 1965.

Under such circumstances, the price of "victory" is indeed high. It will require a rising tempo of slaughter of human beings in Vietnam: people who have been, to allude to the title of Camus' famous essay, the "victims" of a succession of "executioners," all killing people for what they consider sufficient or even noble reasons. Responsibility for this tragedy rests on many shoulders, but as Americans we must face the reality of the suffering and death to which millions of human beings who happen to be Vietnamese are being subjected. In South Vietnam the number of refugees fleeing into coastal areas and Saigon had, by November 1965, reportedly reached nearly three-quarters of a million people. Some among them are fleeing from Vietcong terror, but by the testimony of American[3] and neutral observers alike, the majority are refugees from American napalm bombing and strafing. The Vietcong do not have the means to carry out such mass destruction.

The price of "victory" also means burning and killing for every foot of new ground gained between the Camau Peninsula and the 17th parallel. To subdue and "pacify" the Vietnamese means committing a huge ground army and undertaking massive "counterinsurgency," an antiseptic rubric that in plain English means putting a torch to some villages that may be potential guerrilla sniper spots, destroying rice crops by spraying herbicides from the air, dropping grenades in tunnels that may be full of women and children, bribing children to reveal the location of hideouts, and torturing prisoners to gain information.

The final price of "victory" is the virtual certainty of increased alienation from the Vietnamese people. There is ample evidence that the South Vietnamese view the National Liberation Front with some disaffection because of its terrorism, depredations, heavy taxes, impressment of young men, and continued deferment of the benefits it has promised to bestow. Large numbers of people in the cities and certain rural areas have continued to support the Saigon government and have resisted the appeal to join in the

[3] Statement of former Assistant Secretary of State Roger Hilsman, Professor of Government, Columbia University, New York, New York. Hearings before the Subcommittee to Investigate Problems Connected with Refugees and Escapees of the Committee on the Judiciary, United States Senate, September 30, 1965.

revolutionary movement. But it is also true that the propaganda
efforts of the National Liberation Front had ready-made opportunities to identify American involvement in Vietnam as a continuation of the French colonial enterprise. The Vietnamese vil-
lager knows about American support for the French, for Diem,
and now for the present Saigon government. Who can blame him
for feeling a special resentment toward the white foreigner whose
presence spells massive destruction and economic chaos?

Nor can such alienation and resentment be significantly countered by the positive efforts to provide technical aid and assistance
being made by the United States Agency for International Development (AID) and by some military men. For years the United
States has tried to help the poor of Vietnam through programs of
positive action. AID has struggled, sometimes heroically, to provide educational facilities, improve agricultural techniques, contribute to public health, and strengthen the economy. But the
effort has not changed attitudes significantly, because it has been
so small compared to military activity and because it has been
thwarted by the conditions under which it has had to be done, not
the least of which is the lack of support from the Saigon government. For these positive efforts by the United States to succeed in
providing a foundation for a popularly based political alternative
to the National Liberation Front, there would need to be widespread reforms in land tenure and a thorough cleaning out of corruption. Apparently neither has been possible. United States AID
officials have had to work with a series of regimes that owe their
support to much the same vested interests that were associated
with the government of the French puppet emperor Bao Dai.
Ironically, it is the small group in power that benefits from the
accelerated conflict and the rising cost of living which, at the same
time, increase the despair of the majority.

The continued attempts to combine military and social programs under various guises, from "strategic hamlets" to "pacifica-
tion," achieve no net gain, despite those soldiers and civilians who
have been able to render sincere and devoted service to the people
in certain areas. It is simply not possible to build a house and
burn it at the same time. It is not possible to build a peacetime
society in a land ravaged by civil war and foreign occupation.

The staggering odds against civilian efforts for reconstruction are illustrated in an article in the *Wall Street Journal* of December 16, 1965, where an AID representative is quoted as saying, "The Pentagon is spending more for just its air strip and docks at Cam Ranh Bay than we've been allocated for the nation's entire reconstruction."

Therefore, continuation or escalation of the fighting by the United States, and the almost certain Vietcong reaction, seems likely to produce only increasing alienation and resentment among the people on all sides and will continue to nullify any positive efforts to improve the lot of the Vietnamese or to win their allegiance. These considerations raise an ugly question: even if we win the war, will we lose the peace, because those who survive will hate us?

In other words, can the United States, by applying its global military power, be the champion of the "free" in Vietnam? A glance back at our own historical origins shows the paradox of our present position. Not so long ago we Americans were scattered settlers, colonists creating a new nation concerned with independence. In spite of ties to European motherlands, our founding fathers wanted to be left alone. They were aware that some regarded them as backward, inexperienced, unfit to govern themselves— but they were confident and often brash. In this determined spirit they responded to acts of colonial repression from Britain with a declaration of independence and a violent revolution. The new government was determined to keep the whole western hemisphere free from European interference or domination. Its motto was "no entangling alliances."

Now there is not a spot left in the world where American power and influence do not enter into the calculations of national decision makers. The American presence in Vietnam is a part of this decisive fact of modern life. Under our present policy, many Vietnamese do not even have a voice in deciding whether the war in which they are involved will ever end. It is openly admitted that the Saigon government could not exist without the massive support our government is now providing. To much of the world we, beneficiaries of revolution, appear to be engaged in the forceful suppression of a nationalistic independence movement.

The course of history has brought the United States not only
to a dominant position in military power, but also to a place of
prime responsibility in the conquest of some of humanity's age-old
problems. Most Americans live on a scale far above that of the
multitudes of human beings throughout history. We could devote
ourselves to wiping out poverty in our own country and in other
parts of the world. Instead we find ourselves caught in a miserable
struggle, using our military power to contradict the basic elements
of our own dream of "life, liberty, and the pursuit of happiness"
for all.

At the same time, military expenditures threaten to unbalance
the American economy with attendant risks of inflation. The escalation of the war diverts resources needed to end poverty, to improve our schools, and to halt the deterioration of our cities. A
statement by the assistant chief of the Office of Economic Opportunity, Joseph Kershaw, on December 6, 1965, reveals this situation: "If the military budget goes up anything like what most
people suspect, many of the Great Society projects will have to
be severely cut back, if not abandoned."

In addition to this, the continuation of war constitutes a threat
to our American institutions and the quality of American life.
Many people will somehow cling tenaciously to the tradition of
criticism and individual conscience. The right to dissent has not
yet been drastically curbed. We are not yet completely locked in
what Martin Buber called "the speechlessness of slaughter" that
characterizes war. We are drifting in this direction, however; and
if the war spreads, the trend toward silencing dissent will accelerate
correspondingly with all the dangers that such silencing entails.

Thus the paradox—at the very moment of our greatest hope,
we find ourselves confronted by our gravest danger. The United
States presence in Vietnam perpetuates a spiral of cause and effect
that threatens to engulf the entire world in a war of such scope
and destructiveness that the very fate of mankind hangs in the
balance. The war has already spread to Laos, where we are attack-
ing supply routes, and to Thailand, where American bases are the
major origin for raids on North Vietnam; and Cambodia lies on
the brink. If war continues to spread, the ultimate intervention of
China appears increasingly likely in spite of the probability of

American nuclear retaliation. At the same time, our carefully constructed détente with the Soviet Union in Europe, after showing promise, is lost in a new cold war wave as that country finds itself, no matter how reluctantly, drawn further and further into the war.

Is there any way to escape this dismal entanglement, any way which returns the future of Vietnam to the Vietnamese and offers some prospect for peace and stability in Southeast Asia? Certainly there is no easy formula to assure such a result, but there may be initiatives open to us that offer more hope than the barren cycle of mutual retaliation that characterizes the tactics of escalation. Before such initiatives can be formulated, however, it is important to analyze the underlying forces that are shaping events in Vietnam, for no solution will be viable that does not take these into account.

We therefore turn to a consideration in the next chapters of the three realities that dominate the Southeast Asian scene: the rise of nationalism, the drive for social revolution, and the advent of a militant and reawakened China. When these forces have been explored, we can attempt to assess the adequacy of recent United States policies in Vietnam and to arrive at positive recommendations for a more hopeful future.

2: Nationalism in Southeast Asia

The American government has so consistently imposed its own cold war views and values upon interpretations of developments in Southeast Asia that the American people are not aware of how profoundly the international viewpoints and ideological priorities of most of the people of this area differ from those expressed by the United States.

Throughout Southeast Asia, with the possible exception of Laos, nationalism has been by far the most important political factor. Its appeal has decisively overshadowed that of Communism or anti-Communism. Nationalism has provided the most important barrier to the growth of Communism or the influence of outside Communist powers, and it has been much more effective in countering intervention than any action or lack of action so far taken by the United States.

There has been one exception to this pattern: Vietnam. There, outside pressures have been so overwhelmingly powerful that nationalism has fused with Communism. If we generalize from Vietnam about the rest of Southeast Asia, we violate the facts of recent history.

Yet the administration calls Vietnam "a critical test of the Communist technique of military subversion" and says that if America fails this test, Communists throughout the underdeveloped world will be emboldened to take up arms in attempts to seize power. Such a view, sometimes referred to as the "domino theory," as-

12

sumes that Communists elsewhere lack relevant local experience to guide them and naively regard their own domestic conditions as so similar to those in Vietnam that they must await the outcome of this test before proceeding. But, as Senator Church has stated, "Communist guerrilla wars did not begin in Vietnam and won't end there, regardless of the outcome of this particular struggle." If more American policy makers were better versed in the recent history of Southeast Asia, they might appreciate the fact that the series of Communist "wars of liberation," begun in 1948 in Burma, Indonesia, the Philippines, and Malaya, all failed—and failed decisively. The major reason in each case was that the insurrectionists were unable to secure significant nationalist support and, in fact, ran counter to the mainstream of nationalism. As a consequence, Communist leaders learned more than a decade ago that no insurrection in Southeast Asia can succeed unless it comes to terms with local nationalism.

American postwar policy has been characterized by constant warnings of the danger of Communist Chinese expansionism. Yet the people of Southeast Asia look back over the past decade and see that the power which has most frequently intervened to influence their political destinies has been the United States. In every state of Southeast Asia, America's political presence has been clearly evident, and America's military presence has been infinitely more visible and formidable than that of Communist China or the Soviet Union. In the one area that Americans know well, the Philippines, this intervention has been reasonably consistent with political realities, and relatively enlightened and effective. But the people of Burma and Indonesia, and, to a lesser extent, of Cambodia, are alienated already by American meddling in their domestic affairs. America's military presence in Vietnam has made them even more apprehensive. Indonesia, which incorporates nearly half of Southeast Asia's area and population, and strategically located Burma have come to fear the threat of American political and military interference far more than that of Communist China or the Soviet Union. Although largely unknown to the American public, United States intervention in their affairs has been both recent and flagrant. The strong adverse reaction of the Burmese and Indonesians is only human. Both governments have sup-

PEACE IN VIETNAM

14

pressed Communist insurgencies on their own initiative. The last
thing they want is American support in their efforts. They fear that
such American involvement would boomerang, weakening their
own public support and providing local Communists with more
substantial local backing.

Indonesians of all political views have long been persuaded that
Ho Chi Minh is the genuine voice of Vietnamese nationalism and
the man whom most Vietnamese, South as well as North, would
prefer to support if given the chance. They see many affinities between their own armed struggle against the Dutch and that of the
Vietnamese against the French. Moreover, their attitude toward
American policies is strongly influenced by the United States encouragement and backing of anti-Sukarno rebels in Sumatra and
Celebes in 1957-58. United States Central Intelligence Agency activities involved sea- and air-borne supplies of military equipment
to the rebels, and CIA pilots flew for rebel forces in the bombing of
Indonesian naval vessels and the city of Ambon. Such American
intrusion into national affairs—well known in Indonesia, but little
known by the American public—has had an enduring effect upon
Indonesia's attitude toward the United States and has heightened
its sensitivity to American intervention anywhere in Southeast
Asia, including Vietnam. Opposition to United States policy in
Vietnam is shared by all Indonesian groups—anti-Communist as
well as pro-Communist. Americans who applauded Indonesian
Defense Minister General Nasution's crackdown on the Indonesian
Communist Party beginning in October 1965 well may ponder
the fact that he and his military colleagues are strongly critical of
American military support of the Saigon government.

The Burmese, whose country was the most devastated in all of
Southeast Asia by the fighting in World War II, are sensitive to
the situation in Vietnam and anxious to escape such a fate themselves. They have now secured what they consider an eminently
fair boundary settlement with the People's Republic of China, with
China waiving previous territorial demands. Such a settlement is
one which Chiang Kai-shek's government was never prepared to
countenance and which, in fact, it explicitly repudiated. Of equal
importance to the Burmese leaders, the United States subordi-
nated Burmese national interests to its anti-China policy in the

years before 1961 and encouraged and provided a continuing supply of arms to the forces of Chiang Kai-shek which ravaged Northeast Burma from 1950 to 1961. On the other hand, the Burmese remain grateful that Peking refused to regard the basing of Chiang Kai-shek's troops in northeast Burma as a pretext for sending Chinese Communist forces into Burma after them, even though Chiang Kai-shek's troops made a few probes into China in the early 1950's. This has understandably influenced the Burmese view of current and potential American policy toward China and Vietnam. It is ironic, but true, that for years the American-supported Chinese Nationalist (*Kuomintang*) forces in Burma kept the Burmese government so preoccupied that they could not deal effectively with their country's own dissident Communist groups.

Not only Burma and Indonesia are concerned about American involvement. Having seen the devastation and the casualties inflicted upon the civilian public in Vietnam by America's anti-Communist actions, people in other Southeast Asian countries are anxious to escape such "protection." As the *New York Times* said in its editorial of November 21, 1965, "Even in Thailand and other countries under constant Communist threat, there may be second thoughts about whether conquest by Communists would be more painful than defense by Americans."

The attitudes of Southeast Asian countries toward American anti-Communist policies and, particularly, toward American hostility to Peking have been affected not merely by distrust of the United States and its postwar record of intrusion into their political life. Much more relevant to the national interests of the peoples of Southeast Asia than cold war issues are the traditional quarrels between the individual countries, often originating centuries before the colonial period, but in several cases exaggerated by or actually born from colonial experience. For example, the intense Cambodian antipathy toward Thailand and Vietnam arises from the fact that these states annexed sizable parts of Cambodian territory in the last century and even today control a large number of Cambodian people. This annexation helps explain why the American arming of South Vietnam and Thailand causes such anxiety to Prince Sihanouk of Cambodia. It is also the reason, despite his anti-Communist internal policies, he seeks an accommodation with Communist China to serve as a counterpoise to American backing of South Vietnam and Thailand. Sihanouk would prefer to see American power remain available for deployment in the general area of Southeast Asia, with the Seventh Fleet in a position to deter the Chinese should they ever consider sending their armies across his borders; yet he is convinced that the imminent and palpable threats to his kingdom come from the Vietnamese and Thai armies rather than from those of Communist China. Cambodia has consistently supplied abundant proof of its ability to control Communist internal subversion, for the leadership has been in full harmony with the country's nationalism and has taken steps in social and economic reform that undercut Communist appeals. Indeed, all those who tend to regard American power and American dollars as the best weapons against Communist subversion might note that Cambodia, which has rejected both, continues to maintain a level of internal security unmatched in Southeast Asia.

Sihanouk's confidence in the United States is limited by his belief that the CIA once worked with the Thai and South Vietnamese to overthrow him. He was keenly disappointed at the refusal of the United States to support his proposal for an international conference aimed at providing an international guarantee of Cambodia's borders—a decision the United States later regretted. Cambodian leaders will continue to feel insecure about their border with Vietnam, whether that country is controlled by Communists or anti-Communists. There remains scope for an enlightened and realistic American policy toward Cambodia so long as this is concerned with Cambodia's territorial integrity as such, and not as something subordinate to American cold war plans.

In Thailand, the king remains the symbol of Thai nationalism and the monarchy still works closely with the military and bureaucratic elite of Bangkok. Whatever the shortcomings of the Bangkok regime, Thai nationalism has not been and still appears not to be in danger from any competing form of Thai leadership, and the Communists have made no significant inroads. If the Thai government can be induced to take steps to convince the Lao-speaking majority of northeast Thailand that they are no longer regarded as second-class citizens, there is little likelihood of significant Communist gains. Promised American assistance in developing the resources of the Mekong River Valley may not yet be feasible in Vietnam or in parts of Laos, because of security conditions, but there is plenty of scope for such development in Thailand's economically backward northeast regions. If the Bangkok government can be encouraged to couple reform of local administration with such economic development, Lao-speaking agents of any Communist regime will find little basis for stirring up political dissidence. Communists would undoubtedly have even less reason to intrude if the great American airbase at Udorn in northeast Thailand were not being used for American bombing runs into Laos and North Vietnam. Time has by no means run out in Thailand. As in Cambodia, there is opportunity for enlightened American policies to produce fruitful results.

In considering Laos, we must keep in mind the fact that approximately half the territory is already under the control of pro-Communist elements, the Pathet Lao. We must also acknowledge that the area we refer to as Laos has never constituted a nation. If one uses linguistic and cultural criteria in speaking of a Laotian nationalism, there are at least four times as many Lao in Thailand as in Laos. The Lao-speaking half of the population of Laos is concentrated almost exclusively in the western half of the country, adjacent to Thailand, and especially in the Mekong Valley. Ethnic, linguistic, and historical ties incline this element toward Thai and away from Vietnamese influence. On the other hand, most of the non-Lao, hill-dwelling peoples have generally sought to resist Lao efforts at overlordship, and many of them have close ethnic and linguistic affinities with non-Vietnamese minority groups across the border in Vietnam.

The possibility for a really viable neutralist regime embracing all of Laos, such as Prime Minister Souvanna Phouma endeavored to establish in 1957-58, has now been lost. In the last few years Souvanna Phouma has had good reason to criticize North Vietnam and China for their support of the Communist-oriented Pathet Lao—the Laotian group that has become the major rival to his government. But he cannot be expected to forget that, although the United States in 1961 finally came around to supporting the neutralist government that he had been trying for so long to establish, from 1956 to 1958 it had openly undertaken to subvert and topple his government by supporting the right-wing factions under General Phoumi Nosovan. The Thai government, which joined the United States in backing Phoumi Nosovan, has continued to oppose the establishment of a neutralist Laos. This has not made Souvanna Phouma's subsequent efforts any easier. Whatever the settlement in Vietnam, the several ethnic components of Laos are likely to gravitate in the same directions they did prior to their artificial administrative unification by France.

Clearly the force of nationalism in the countries of Southeast Asia does not justify any simple "domino-theory" approach in United States policy toward that area. The power of this nationalism will remain the watchful guardian of political independence, poised against any hint of outside interference—whether from China or the United States. As long as Southeast Asian governments are in harmony with their countries' nationalism and so long as they prove capable, wise, and strong enough to institute the basic reforms necessary to meet the most pressing socioeconomic demands of their peoples, indigenous Communist leaders are likely to encounter little success.

How well is the United States relating to these demands for social revolution and thereby contributing to the security and stability of the newly emerging nations of Southeast Asia?

3: The Need for Socioeconomic Change in Southeast Asia

Too often, in the complexities of the Vietnam situation itself, we forget that since World War II a greater percentage of the world's wealth has become concentrated in the hands of a smaller percentage of the earth's population than ever before. Although there has been some absolute increase in production in the predominantly agrarian countries of eastern Asia, the increase is small compared with the rapid growth in population and the rising expectations of an increasingly aware populace. Paul Martin, Canada's Secretary of State for External Affairs, outlined the general problem in a speech given in Cleveland, Ohio, in September 1964:

In the decade from 1950 to 1960 the countries of the underdeveloped world were able to increase their production of goods and services from $110 billion to just under $170 billion. This means that at the beginning of the decade as at the end of it, these countries accounted for only three-tenths of all the goods and services produced in the free world as a whole. Over the same period the total population of these countries increased from one thousand million to thirteen hundred million people. That is a rate almost twice as high as that experienced in the advanced countries of the free world. When the growth of production is discounted by the growth of population, we find that the less developed countries were able to increase their average per

19

capita income over the decade by no more than $25, from $105 in
1950 to $130 in 1960. In other words per capita income in these
countries rose by a mere $2.50 a year. What is more significant is
that during this ten-year period, the gap between standards of living
in these countries and standards of living in the advanced countries
widened in both absolute and relative terms.[1]

Naturally conditions of livelihood and economic growth in the
underdeveloped countries of Asia vary from country to country
and from area to area within countries. The situation in Thailand
and Burma with their general rice surplus is clearly better than
that of India, where food shortages are approaching catastrophic
proportions. Also the rich delta area of southern Thailand presents
a different picture from that of its impoverished northeast. But
these are relative differences and temporary advantages. In none
of these countries has a modern economy developed. In varying
degrees they all are dominated by traditional patterns of agrarian
subsistence economy. Land is the essential element of wealth, and
what little private capital is accumulated is usually invested in
buying more land, in usury, or in commodity speculation. Seldom
is it put to work as productive capital beyond making minimal
improvements in land or processing techniques.

The preceding chapter showed that nationalism is the prime
mover in the emancipation from colonial rule. The need and demand for socioeconomic innovation accompanies nationalism and
becomes more insistent as time goes by. It must necessarily be a
dominant preoccupation of any new national government. The
United States must learn to deal with this and welcome its constructive aspects.

In remarks to editors and broadcasters attending a national
foreign policy conference in Washington on April 21, 1964, President Johnson said:

Poverty, hunger, and disease are afflictions as old as man himself.
But in our time and in this age there has been a change. The change
is not so much in the realities of life, but in the hopes and expectations of the future. If a peaceful revolution in these areas is impossible,
a violent revolution is inevitable.

[1] *Vital Speeches of the Day,* October 15, 1965, p. 31.

However, in facing this problem, just as in facing the question of nationalism in Southeast Asia, the United States government has consistently guided its activities with an overriding concern to "stop Communism." In order to deal with the demands for socioeconomic revolution and also contain Communism, Washington has evolved a two-pronged approach: economic assistance and military assistance with special emphasis on counterinsurgency programs. This approach is based in part on theories of economic growth propounded by Walt W. Rostow, now chairman of the State Department Policy Planning Council. According to Mr. Rostow, there are several stages in the transition from the traditional agrarian economy to modern industrialism with its high mass consumption. At the beginning this transition is a slow process requiring the accumulation of vast amounts of capital. When sufficient capital has been accumulated or poured into the country from the outside, its economy reaches a take-off stage. At this point the various elements of the economy—capital accumulation, entrepreneurial drives, labor skills, technology—all accelerate rapidly, thus leading to a stage of self-sustaining growth. Then the country is well on its way toward the development of a modern industrial society.

The countries of eastern and southern Asia encompassed in the vast crescent arch extending from Korea to Pakistan, with the exceptions of Japan, Singapore, and probably Taiwan, are all still in the pre-take-off stage, or just beginning to enter it.

In the view of Rostow and other foreign policy planners in Washington, this is a period fraught with danger, since needs and desires tend to outrun the capacity to satisfy them, and the resulting discontent leads to political instability. It is at this point that Communism has its opportunity to gain ascendancy. Therefore, as we pour capital and technical assistance into these countries in order to speed up the process of economic modernization, we also help friendly governments develop counterinsurgency programs on a large scale. By so doing, it is hoped that stability can be maintained through the take-off stage, usually a period of a decade or two, and that the Communists will be thwarted in their attempt to gain power during the intervening period.

Our two-pronged approach of economic assistance and counter-

insurgency, however, involves a fatal contradiction. Transition to
the stage of self-sustaining growth requires three elements: capital
accumulation, technical innovation, and institutional change. The
latter includes such matters as land reform, a switch from subsistence to commercial crops, the widespread establishment of
credit, supply and marketing cooperatives, expanded educational
opportunities, population control, and the introduction of modern
accounting methods and fiscal responsibility in government. It also
necessitates the curtailment of privileges, favoritism, and corruption—hallmarks of traditional Asian political systems.

Without this institutional change the pouring in of capital and
technical assistance from outside can, at best, produce only a thin
veneer of urban modernization superimposed on a backward,
underdeveloped, and increasingly frustrated society. Indigenous
capital accumulation remains extremely difficult, and increased
production based on improvements in agriculture and in local in-
dustries fails to materialize.

All of these changes have been goals of stated American policy,
but the problem lies in gaining the cooperation of local ruling
groups in overcoming vested interests and the inertia of the old
society. In the past our chief hopes for bringing about change have
rested with the newly emerging, modern-minded, Western-oriented
middle class in these countries; wherever possible we have supported this class and the middle-of-the-road governments led by it.

Unfortunately this class is small in numbers and almost entirely
confined to the major cities. It has practically no political strength
at all in the vast countryside where most of the population live.
All too frequently the real political power lies with a group
made up of traditional land-based gentry, a closely associated
military caste, and urban merchants who are tied to the traditional
socioeconomic pattern and strongly opposed to any change in the
status quo that affects their immediate interests. Also allied with
this group are many vestigial colonial interests: plantation owners,
mine operators, lumber and petroleum firms, and other foreign
concerns that produce raw materials for world markets.

The chief potential counter-force, aside from a small and highly
volatile section of the urban student and working-class population,
consists largely of the mass of frustrated peasantry and ethnic or

religious minorities who feel themselves oppressed under the status quo. The peasantry, although a numerical majority, has heretofore lived in a state of tradition-bound political apathy and local isolation. When conditions became intolerable, it was capable of reaction in the form of local riots but was rarely able to mount an organized mass movement with broad political and social programs. Now, however, the situation is changing. With the great advance in communications, the peasantry is becoming more aware of the world around it, the possibilities of political action, and particularly the power of organization. The demand of these people for change makes them sympathetic to revolutionary programs; programs that promise the social services and material goods that signify a fuller, more comfortable life. The lesson of organization for such programs is usually provided by those most interested in mass revolutionary change on the peasant level, i.e., Communist or non-Communist left-wing groups. It is important to point out that these groups, although they receive moral support from some Communist countries, derive their basic support from peasant and worker discontent and are led primarily by idealistic intellectuals from the middle class.

Thus, as the existing national governments come under increasing pressure from their people to institute socioeconomic reforms, change will be inevitable. And since the need has already reached a critical point in most of these countries, only a stable, highly organized government with strong powers seems to be capable of carrying out such reforms. In some places this power may take the form of a left-wing or even Communist government. But this does not necessarily mean that a militantly anti-American bloc will emerge. Surely a major factor is the attitude of the United States toward these new regimes. By pursuing a two-pronged policy which, on the one hand, claims to seek peace, stability, and progress for the area but which, on the other hand, has as its overriding concern the stopping of Communism, the United States is usually obliged to support those committed to maintaining the status quo, thus almost assuring the very kind of violent and anti-American revolution that it most seeks to prevent.

On the other hand, if the United States, recognizing the inevitability of change and the natural development of a socio-

economic revolution in an area, can offer constructive aid free
from the threat of accompanying political or military intervention,
the governments it is dealing with can develop independently in
the spirit of the nationalism that gave them their first impetus.

The example of eastern Europe illustrates the importance of
United States policy in this matter. A gradual development of
more or less independent attitudes in international affairs on the
part of the eastern European countries came after the Hungarian
revolt in 1956. The failure of the United States to intervene at the
time demonstrated that it was not prepared to carry through with
its previously declared intention to assist in the "liberation" of
the "captive nations." Thus not only have the leaders of these
countries felt less compelled to seek the protection of the Soviet
Union, but the Soviet Union itself has been more willing to relax
its hold over them. As a result, the tendency toward extreme po-
larization in Europe, represented by NATO and the Warsaw Pact,
has been eased, and the chances for peace in Europe now appear
greater than at any time since World War II. Increased independence on the part of eastern European countries, although
made possible by these circumstances, stems primarily from their
divergent national interests. No matter what ideological ties may
exist between Communists, once a Communist party is in power,
it finds itself moved to meet the needs of its own people apart
from the interest of the associated Communist countries as a
whole. The obvious reluctance of both the Soviet Union and the
eastern European countries to commit themselves to all-out support of the North Vietnamese and National Liberation Front stems
in large measure from this fact.

Some may demur that to suggest abandonment of present American policy in Southeast Asia in favor of an all-out emphasis on
constructive socioeconomic aid is an oversimplification of the problems involved. They well may ask whether it is possible that the
United States need only withdraw its support of status quo regimes
in order to have them give way to progressive governments ready
and able to bring about immediate socioeconomic revolutions, and
at the same time willing to seek the aid of the United States. Of
course the process is by no means so simple. The task facing any
government committed to bringing about fundamental change in

the underdeveloped countries of Asia is so enormous that it is certain to involve a long, difficult, and often extremely bitter process. Left-wing or Communist regimes in themselves do not constitute any passport to rapid economic progress. Neither China nor the Soviet Union has escaped serious errors in the process of industrialization, particularly in regard to the extremely complicated problem of maintaining a proper balance between industrial and agricultural development. However, these have generally been errors committed in the process of growth—a growth possible only after the elimination of the restraints imposed by the old socioeconomic patterns. In this growth both countries have shown a real responsiveness to the needs of the people. The rise in the general standard of living, literacy, and health has been spectacular, compared with those countries still following an old social order. An example can be cited from North Vietnam in 1956, where an effort to apply unsuitable Chinese patterns of agrarian reform in one province resulted in peasant rioting. Army troops sternly subdued the incipient rebellion. The particular reform was then abandoned for more suitable methods and President Ho Chi Minh removed the pro-Chinese official who had administered it. Revolutionary social change has so far always exacted a cost in terms of human lives and misery. This cost must be seen in relation to the alternative of extending the hunger, disease, ignorance, and chronic violence of the past into an overpopulated and overarmed world of the future.

Many Asians are now heaping the onus of Western imperialism on American shoulders. This accusation is not without some justification and cannot easily be shed. Any new revolutionary government that comes to power in Asia will probably begin with virulent denunciations of the United States, if only to prove that it is upholding the cause of anti-imperialism. American-owned businesses may suffer and may be nationalized, and Americans and their friends will certainly find life less comfortable than before. How long would it be before national interests would lead these governments to seek some accommodation with the United States? This will be governed by how long and in what measure the United States continues to pose a threat. Algeria is a case in point. When finally allowed to develop as an independent nation,

Algeria quickly sought the aid of the United States and even France, and today American and French enterprises play a widening role in the economic development of that country.

This analysis of revolutionary political and socioeconomic movements points to the fact that the old days of military dominance of Asian countries by white Western powers is over. Economic assistance through trade, loans, and direct aid is more pertinent than ever, provided it does not jeopardize the newly won political independence. An interesting recognition of the new era comes from the British Tory defense spokesman Enoch Powell, who stated at a conference of the Conservative Party on October 14, 1965, that Britain's military commitment east of Suez should be abandoned because it is self-defeating at some points.[2]

The United States has not yet acknowledged this new era. The reason given for its continuing military commitment is that Southeast Asia must be defended from Chinese Communist encroachment. The potential role of China in this area must therefore be considered.

[2] *New York Times,* October 15, 1965.

4: The Role of China

The American public seems to be thoroughly convinced that China is the "Number One Enemy" in Asia. Talk of a preventive war to wipe out China's nuclear potential is prevalent now just as it was during the early 1950's in regard to the Soviet Union. South Vietnamese often privately complain that, though it is their people who are being killed and their country that is being devastated, the real object of the American military effort is China. Yet there is no indication that so much as a single Chinese has been involved in the fighting so far.

What then can we say about China? Is this a country bent on establishing a Chinese-dominated, Communist empire in Asia through political subversion and outright military conquest? In that case who can talk of independent nationalism or of revolutionary governments making accommodations with the United States?

First of all, it must be stated clearly that any speculation based either on subjective prejudices or wishful thinking concerning just what the Chinese will or will not do in any specific situation is dangerous. President Truman and General MacArthur, with all the intelligence resources available during the Korean War, proved to be terribly wrong when they arbitrarily chose to ignore Chinese warnings against American troops crossing the 38th parallel and approaching Chinese borders in the autumn of 1950.

Yet it is possible to make some valid observations concerning

Chinese foreign policy and intentions if we are willing to cut through her verbose hostility, distinguish between her general propaganda and specific statements of policy, and at the same time check these against what she is actually doing. Certainly the Chinese are going through a period of militant nationalism that accounts for much of their bellicosity. At the same time, the Chinese leaders believe their revolutionary experience constitutes a model for other underdeveloped countries. But in spite of this seemingly extreme orientation, their specific activities have been tempered by rather conservative guidelines. For example, in terms of both specific statements and actions, the Chinese have been extremely cautious in dealing with the United States. They have gone to some lengths to avoid any direct confrontation with this country, even permitting American convoys of ships to carry Nationalist Chinese troops to Quemoy under their very guns. Furthermore, although the Chinese have adhered consistently to certain demands, such as their insistence that Taiwan is an internal problem that must be settled without any foreign interference, they have demonstrated considerable flexibility in dealing with many questions of policy.

The chief elements of Chinese foreign policy can be listed as follows:

1. The Chinese insist that all boundary or territorial concessions resulting from the unequal treaties imposed upon China by the colonial powers during the nineteenth and twentieth centuries be renegotiated. Recently new boundary agreements have been negotiated with the now independent countries of Afghanistan, Pakistan, Nepal, Burma, and Outer Mongolia under terms that more or less preserved the status quo and were generally fair to all parties. As yet there has been no boundary settlement with the Soviet Union, India including Sikkhim and Bhutan, Laos, or Vietnam. The Chinese are respecting the terms of the agreements they inherited concerning Hong Kong and Macao, and are not pushing for a return of these territories now.

2. The People's Republic of China considers Taiwan to be an integral part of its territory and the Nationalist government to be a remnant "counterrevolutionary force" having no legal status and maintained only through American armed intervention. It insists

the United States must withdraw its forces from the area, but for some time has refrained from any rash action either in regard to Taiwan or the Nationalist-held offshore islands.

3. The Chinese say that since 1950 the United States has been engaged in active aggression against the People's Republic of China, sometimes directly and sometimes through "its puppets," the Nationalists on Taiwan. Prior to that time the United States supplied and often took direct part in Nationalist attempts to suppress the revolution. The United States is also regarded as having done everything possible to impede the Chinese economic construction through blockades, embargoes, and general pressure to isolate mainland China from the rest of the world. Therefore, the Chinese feel that in the interest of national security they cannot tolerate the presence on their borders of any American forces or of forces under American domination. Such presence will be met with military force, as happened in Korea and was threatened in Laos.

4. The Chinese feel that any government in eastern Asia which permits itself to become an outpost of American military power poses a threat to the peace of Asia and at least indirectly to the security of China. Chinese attitudes toward these countries vary with specific circumstances. Pakistan and Thailand are both members of SEATO, but there was considerable difference in the Chinese attitude toward them even before the development of the Sino-Indian dispute. Governments such as those in Thailand and South Vietnam, which are associated with American military ventures involving Chinese interests, are treated as hostile, and the Chinese give active support, including arms, financial aid, and other forms of assistance, to the left-wing movements attempting to overthrow them. Thailand has recently become a special target because of the extensive American airbases there that are used in bombing North Vietnam. The Chinese are less sensitive to American military activity in noncontiguous nations such as the Philippines.

5. Where countries on China's borders have taken a definitely neutral stand, the Chinese have adopted a policy of general non-interference even to the disadvantage of strong dissident left-wing groups, such as exist within Burma and Nepal.

6. Throughout the rest of the underdeveloped world, the Chi-

nese have used propaganda and aid in attempts to influence these countries toward "anti-imperialist" and specifically anti-American policies. They have also carried on propaganda activities and given moral support to dissident elements in countries that have adopted strong pro-Western positions. In some places, such as the Congo and Algeria, where revolutionary warfare had broken out, they have supplied limited material assistance as well.

Thus, even though the Chinese consider themselves faithful Marxist-Leninists, their policies in actual practice have been shaped much more by immediate national concerns. They view the United States as an implacable enemy and their policies and activities have been directed more *against it* than *for* any program for world revolution or the creation of some new Chinese empire. China's three major military ventures since 1949 have dealt with such national concerns. In Tibet it reasserted a long-standing Chinese claim to sovereignty—a claim which is asserted also by the Chinese Nationalist government of Taiwan.[1] Its participation in the Korean War was directed against what it felt to be an immediate American threat to its security. The military conflict with India certainly involved invasion of another country, but was a limited action taken for the purpose of forcing a settlement of a frontier dispute.

Furthermore, the Chinese military establishment, although possessed of tremendous manpower resources, is extremely limited in offensive weapons and the kind of logistical support necessary for any strong action outside its borders. It is also the almost unanimous view of observers on the spot that, as Charles Taylor, Peking correspondent for the *Toronto Globe and Mail,* says,[2] the Chinese are now primarily concerned with economic growth and other internal problems rather than with militarism.

Clearly what China would like to see, at least for the present,

[1] The Chinese Nationalist delegate to the United Nations Security Council in November 1950 pointed out during the discussion of the Tibetan question that Tibet had been a part of China for seven hundred years and had participated in the National Assembly of 1946 to draft the new constitution as well as in that of 1948 to elect the President and Vice-President. See Tieh-Tseng Li, *The Historical Status of Tibet* (New York: King's Crown Press, 1956).

[2] *The Nation,* October 4, 1965.

is an intermediate zone around her borders consisting of generally friendly or at least neutral countries. Such a zone would not necessarily be contrary to the interests of the United States. It would continue to be an area in which Western and Chinese influence would compete, but not through subversion or military conquest.

But what about Peking's general warlike attitude, its supposed denial of the principle of co-existence, and its espousal of revolutionary wars of liberation as a means of isolating and weakening "the imperialist" nations? This again needs to be examined carefully, especially since, as one of the main components of the Sino-Soviet dispute, the Chinese position in regard to co-existence has tended to be twisted by both the Soviet and Western spokesmen.

First, the Chinese maintain that they adhere to the principle of co-existence of states with different social systems, and repeatedly assert that they are for peace. But they insist that this does not require any people to accept domination by imperialists or reactionaries or to accept outside aggression. In other words, wars of liberation and wars resisting aggression are "just" wars. Furthermore, they maintain that co-existence applies in different ways to different countries and that different policies must be adopted toward different types such as other socialist countries, nonsocialist countries that have recently attained independence, ordinary capitalist countries, and imperialist countries. The United States falls in a category by itself as the superimperialist power bent on world empire through the establishment of military bases and control of puppet governments throughout the world. With it, the Chinese maintain, no co-existence is possible as long as the United States maintains what they now regard as being a policy of "imperialism and aggression." They criticize the Soviet Union's attempt to obtain peace with the United States through negotiation because they say a lasting peace can only be assured through universal disarmament. Anything short of this, especially in the field of nuclear weapons, simply perpetuates a military monopoly of the big powers. But, they say, universal disarmament is completely unthinkable for the United States at this point for two basic reasons. First, according to their analysis, its economy is based on war production, and disarmament would lead to economic collapse. Second, disarmament would mean an end to American imperialism and its special privileges overseas. Therefore, they reason, the American ruling class could not possibly enter into negotiations for a meaningful peace in good faith, and the best chance of preserving peace, they think, is to weaken imperialism by supporting peace movements in the advanced capitalist countries and liberation movements elsewhere.

In recent months, with the escalation of the war in Vietnam, the Chinese have paid increased attention to the question of liberation movements. In a recent speech commemorating the twentieth anniversary of the victory over Japan, Lin Piao, one of China's leading Communists, addressed himself to this very problem. This speech[3] has received considerable attention because Lin attempts to project the experience of the Chinese Communist guerrilla-type warfare against Japan and the Nationalists in terms of defeating the United States on the world scene. He stresses the fact that, in the face of a strong enemy capable of seizing the big cities and main lines of communication,

the countryside, and countryside alone, can provide the revolutionary bases from which the revolutionaries can go forward to final victory. . . . Taking the entire globe, if North America and Western Europe can be called "the cities of the world," then Asia, Africa and Latin America constitute "the rural areas of the world. . . ." In a sense, the contemporary world revolution also presents a picture of the encirclement of cities by the rural areas.

Thus,

. . . the Socialist countries should regard it as their international duty to support the people's revolutionary struggles in Asia, Africa and Latin America.

At the same time he stresses the fact that these revolutions must be home-grown.

If one does not operate by one's own efforts, does not independently ponder and solve the problems of the revolution in one's own country

[3] *Peking Review*, No. 36, September 3, 1965. An abbreviated version in *New York Times*, September 4, 1965.

and does not rely on the strength of the masses but leans wholly on foreign aid—even though this be aid from Socialist countries which persist in revolution—no victory can be won, or be consolidated even if it is won.

And further on he states,

Of course, every revolution in a country stems from the demands of its own people. Only when the people in a country are awakened, mobilized, organized and armed can they overthrow the reactionary rule of imperialism and its lackeys through struggle; their role cannot be replaced or taken over by any people from outside. In this sense, revolution cannot be imported.

He chides those who may be fearful of American military power by repeating the Chinese argument that, while the United States is strong tactically, it is weak strategically. Its nuclear weapons cannot be lightly used. The more it attempts to suppress revolutionary movements, the more isolated and pinned down it becomes so that it is incapable of concentrating its tactical might. In the words of Mao Tse-tung, "Whenever it commits aggression, it puts a new noose around its neck. It is besieged ring upon ring by the people of the whole world."

This is not very pleasant reading for either the "dove" or the "hawk." For the former it constitutes an acceptance of the use of violence as a necessary method; for the latter it raises again the fear of becoming overextended and bogged down in the morass of an unwinnable Asian war.

But actually the entire Chinese proposition is based on the premise that the United States will continue its present stress on counterinsurgency programs and thus stimulate pressures toward revolution in the various underdeveloped areas of the world, which will assume an anti-American slant. Lin Piao's statement in no way suggests that the Chinese intend to create these revolutions themselves, even supposing they were able, which they definitely are not. Though the Chinese have the capacity to provide some training and material support to revolutionaries, their ability to influence revolutionary movements is primarily ideological and stems from their position as the foremost spokesman of revolution and defiance of the "white West." The success of the Chinese

Communists in transforming China from a weak, backward nation
in the throes of social and economic collapse to a major world
power capable of challenging the might of the United States and,
moreover, being accepted by it as its chief threat to world leadership, cannot help but arouse interest in the rest of the underdeveloped world. And even the most conservative member of the
formerly subjugated colored races tends to enjoy a certain iden-
tification at hearing China's bellicose defiance directed toward
the great white United States. Thus, just as counterinsurgency
tends to intensify the very kind of explosion it seeks to prevent,
so the intensity of American efforts against the People's Republic
of China tends to increase China's prestige in the underdeveloped
areas of the world.

For over two thousand years the people of Vietnam considered the Chinese their chief foreign menace; and though they
were profoundly influenced by Chinese culture—wet rice farming,
political and social institutions, philosophy, law, religion, archi-
tecture, and system of writing—the relations between the two areas
were often marked by fierce struggle. The Chinese dominated much
of the Vietnam area up to the tenth century A.D. Vietnam retained
a certain independence within the Chinese tribute system until
the middle of the nineteenth century, when the French gained
ascendancy largely by supporting local native powers against the
Chinese or Chinese-supported regimes. Again after the defeat of
Japan, Chinese nationalist armies occupied the northern area of
Vietnam, where they incurred further distrust by looting the country and interfering in its domestic policies. In spite of the traditional fear of Chinese domination, however, events since 1950
have forced North Vietnam into an increasing dependence upon
China. Nowhere has the self-defeating nature of American support
for colonial and right-wing anti-Communist regimes become so
apparent as in Vietnam itself.

Relations between Chinese and Vietnamese Communists go
back to 1924, when Ho Chi Minh was sent to Canton as part of
the Third International Advisory Mission to Sun Yat-sen's nationalist movement there. At this time Ho is said to have worked
with Mao Tse-tung in a school for training agrarian revolutionaries
and in the late 1930's to have spent some time in Yenan, capital

of Chinese Communist territory in northwest China. Practical
working relations between Vietnamese and Chinese Communists,
however, did not develop until after the Chinese Communists took
over the mainland of China in 1949. In 1950 the People's Republic of China along with the Soviet Union granted official recognition to the Democratic Republic of Vietnam. Although Chinese
support for Ho Chi Minh's forces in the war against the French
was limited at first, after the end of the Korean War captured
American arms and other aid were sent to Vietnam in significant
amounts. After the Geneva Conference of 1954, the Chinese, and
also the Soviet Union, continued to provide North Vietnam with
technical and material assistance in substantial quantities.

During the early years of the Sino-Soviet dispute, the North
Vietnamese Communists endeavored to assume a neutral position,
clearly hoping to avoid being too closely tied to either party.
Beginning in May 1963, after American activities in South Vietnam were expanded and intensified, the North Vietnamese, while
maintaining close ties with the Soviet Union, commenced to give
more consistent support to the Chinese position.

So far the Chinese have apparently taken no initiative in seeking
any negotiations on Vietnam and have insisted that peace can
come only through an American return to the Geneva Agreement
and acceptance of the four-point basis for peace laid down by
the North Vietnamese. The Chinese have also stated that Chinese
volunteers would be available if requested, and recent press reports
indicate that Chinese technicians and laborers are playing an increasing role in helping the Vietnamese repair damage caused by
American bombing. Though the Chinese are clearly anxious to
avoid a direct confrontation with the United States, any American
invasion of North Vietnam itself would almost certainly bring
them openly into the war.

Thus the course of recent events in Vietnam has served to make
China a more imminent threat to the security and independence
of Southeast Asia than it has been before, and indeed than our
earlier analysis suggests it need be. We see little evidence that
China is likely to embark upon a policy of conquest if American
military forces are withdrawn. China's efforts to influence its
neighbors through traditional instruments of cultural penetration

and economic pressure will surely continue, as they have for centuries. The new countries stand a better chance of retaining independence as a result of their own aroused forces of nationalism than through American military intervention.

5: History of United States Involvement in Vietnam

In most of Southeast Asia, anti-colonial nationalist movements secured independence either peacefully or following a bitter but relatively brief struggle. The notable exception was Vietnam. There, France's wartime policies and her continuing stubborn resistance to the demands of Vietnamese nationalists brought non-Communist and Communist patriots together in a common effort to secure independence.

In their occupation of colonial Southeast Asia during World War II, the Japanese—except in the French colonies—deemed it advantageous to work through elements of the Western educated native élites, regarding them as more reliable than the colonial civil servants. In return for their cooperation in administering the occupied countries, the Japanese usually granted educated nationals higher administrative positions and considerably greater scope for political activities than they had previously enjoyed. The Japanese also made promises of independence and sometimes granted a significant measure of freedom to organize nationalist movements. Nationalist leaders, therefore, usually found it more to their interests to operate above ground, in some sort of marriage of convenience with the Japanese, than to attempt underground resistance.

The one great exception was Indochina (Vietnam, Cambodia,

37

and Laos). Here in 1941 the pro-Vichy French administration promptly came to terms with the Japanese, making an arrangement whereby they were to retain their administrative positions, under general control and supervision of the Japanese. In Vietnam, then, the Japanese were able to rely upon the French and had no need to make concessions to the leading nationalists. Consequently, along with their French collaborators, the Japanese cracked down very hard upon any nationalist activity. Because of this, non-Communist as well as pro-Communist Vietnamese nationalists were forced to operate underground, a level of political activity in which the Communists were already experienced. Thus, even at this early stage, the most important channel open to Vietnamese who wished to free their country from French control was one where Vietnamese Communists already had an entrenched position. Indeed, the only strong and organized underground in existence was that which had been built up by the Vietnamese Communists under the leadership of Ho Chi Minh. Thus most Vietnamese nationalists, regardless of their political convictions, joined. The ability of the various groups to work together was undoubtedly increased by the fact that from the very outset the Vietnamese Communist movement had a strong nationalist bias. Although Ho Chi Minh, the leader of this wide nationalist coalition known as the Vietminh, was a Communist who had spent some time in Russia and China, he held his position by virtue of his nationalism rather than his Communism, as even Ngo Dinh Diem acknowledged.

During World War II the Vietminh received considerable support from Chiang Kai-shek's government and, as the war drew to a close, from the American Office of Strategic Services, forerunner of the CIA. It developed increasing power, and by May 1945 had liberated a part of northern Vietnam from Japanese rule. When Japan capitulated, the Vietminh and supporting groups supplanted the discredited and weakly backed national regime which the Japanese at the eleventh hour had established under Bao Dai, the previous French colonial puppet-emperor of Annam (central Vietnam).

The policies of the French in Vietnam in the period after the war were of even greater importance in causing nationalism to fuse with Communism. Again, Vietnam stood in contrast to the non-French colonial areas of Southeast Asia. For unlike the Americans and British who had the wisdom to grant independence to their colonies, and unlike the less powerful Dutch whom the United States refused to support after 1949, the French remained intransigent. With increasing American support, they continued to resist Vietnamese claims for independence to the very last— down to their military defeat at Dienbienphu in 1954. This unyielding French policy gave Vietnamese nationalists of all political orientations, pro-Communist and non-Communist, no effective alternative but to work together against the French. Thus in Vietnam, in marked contrast to the other countries of Southeast Asia, the mainstream of the nationalist movement came under the domination of a largely Communist leadership; and all Vietnamese recognized Ho Chi Minh's Communist-led Vietminh as the force that successfully opposed French power and eventually secured Vietnamese independence.

Although Franklin Roosevelt had made clear his opposition to any reoccupation of Vietnam by France and had advocated making it a United Nations trusteeship territory, the Truman administration—while hoping France would ultimately grant Vietnam independence—undertook to back French efforts to re-establish control. To avoid antagonizing France, which it was hoped could be made the keystone of an American-sponsored European military alliance, the United States temporized in Vietnam with respect to its general commitment to self-determination. Our support to France increased until we were underwriting two-thirds of the costs of her military effort, with well over a billion dollars allocated in the year 1953 alone. By granting this support, the United States took its first long step toward making the Vietnamese cynical about American protestations of support for national self-determination.

France's military defeat culminated in mid-1954 with Dienbienphu, setting the stage for the Geneva Conference of that year. An understanding of the political failure that accompanied this military defeat is most important to any analysis of the present situation. In 1950 the French had established a Vietnamese regime under Bao Dai. Never given political autonomy, let alone independence, this regime had proved incapable of winning popular support. Most of its administrators were Frenchmen or Vietnamese who were regarded by the population as agents of the French.

At the time of Geneva there were, then, two competing governments. One was the Vietminh government of Ho Chi Minh, controlling about three-quarters of the country, with approximately as much of its territory south as north of the 17th parallel. The other government was the French military administration with its Vietnamese veneer—the essentially puppet government of Bao Dai, operating in French-held enclaves both north and south of the 17th parallel, and largely confined to urban areas such as Hanoi, Saigon, and their immediate surroundings.

The representatives of nine governments participated in the Geneva Conference of 1954: Cambodia, the People's Republic of China, France, Laos, the Democratic Republic of Vietnam (the Vietminh), the State of Vietnam (the French-supported Bao Dai regime), the Union of Soviet Socialist Republics, the United Kingdom, and the United States of America. It is important to note that there were two agreements: The Geneva Accords (Final Declaration) and the Geneva Armistice Agreement (Agreement on the Cessation of Hostilities).[1] The armistice agreement was the essential foundation upon which the Accords rested. It provided for a military truce between two parties only: Ho Chi Minh's Vietminh government and the French military command. The regime of Bao Dai, of which the present Saigon government is successor, was merely the powerless agent of the French military administration. It was the French who disposed of all real authority in those areas not controlled by the Vietminh. This military truce between the French and the Vietminh was the basic document, providing for temporary partition of Vietnam and for the withdrawal of French troops from north, and of Vietminh forces from south, of the 17th parallel.

This partition, however, was clearly described in terms of a military regroupment of forces. It involved no political boundary and certainly provided no basis for the establishment of a separate state in the South. Article 6 of the Final Declaration at Geneva could not have been more explicit: "The Conference recognizes

[1] See Appendix I-A.

that the essential purpose of the agreement relating to Vietnam is to settle military questions with a view to ending hostilities and that the military demarcation line is provisional and should not in any way be interpreted as constituting a political or territorial boundary." [2]

The Vietminh was reluctant to agree to this partition, which left it with slightly less than half of the territory of Vietnam, despite the fact that at the time it controlled three-quarters. However, Ho Chi Minh's government was under strong Soviet and Chinese pressure to give way on this point. The concern of China, and probably also the Soviet Union, was that continuation of the war might cause the introduction of American military power —possibly atomic—in support of the French, a course of action which the United States did in fact come very close to taking. The Vietminh accepted this temporary loss because of the explicit promise in both the armistice agreement and in the Geneva Declaration that within a period of two years national elections would be held to unify the country. They had every reason to believe that these elections would take place because the agreements stipulated that France, the other party to the armistice, was to maintain control of civil administration in the South until elections were held (Article 14a of the armistice agreement). In effect, then, the elections and the military truce were interdependent, a fact often disregarded.

Despite this stipulation, less than a year after the Geneva Conference, France, alleging American pressure, pulled out of Vietnam without honoring its obligations concerning the elections; and the United States stepped in to fill the void left by the departure of French power.

The United States had not been a party to the military truce and had not actually assented to the Geneva Declaration. Informed observers have said that the major reason was the unwillingness of Secretary of State Dulles to appear to give any ground to Communism, especially at the time of an election campaign. Instead, at Geneva the United States had made its own unilateral declaration wherein it undertook to refrain from the threat or use of force to disturb the Geneva Accords. With respect to the pro-

[2] See Appendix I-B.

vision for elections, it had stated: "In the case of nations now divided against their will, we shall continue to seek to achieve unity through elections supervised by the United Nations to insure that they are conducted fairly." [3] In its declaration the United States likewise spoke only of a single Vietnam, not of a South and a North Vietnam.

It was not until January 1955 that France transferred all the essential attributes of authority to the Saigon regime headed by Bao Dai. But even before this the United States had begun to support his administration and especially Prime Minister Ngo Dinh Diem, who had been appointed by Bao Dai two weeks before the Geneva Conference concluded.

Diem came from a Roman Catholic Mandarin family which served the vestigial and effectively French-controlled imperial Annamese court at Hué in central Vietnam. After working in the imperial administration for four years, Diem resigned in 1933 because of a dispute with Emperor Bao Dai. In 1949, following a long period of political retirement and study, Diem was offered the premiership by Ho Chi Minh. He turned it down, in part because he held the Vietminh responsible for the murder of his brother. After an unsuccessful attempt to develop a rival political party, he left Vietnam in August 1950 and spent four years abroad, mostly in the United States. At least as early as November 1954, the United States had decided to support Diem in setting up an anti-Communist state in South Vietnam, making clear that American aid would be given to him alone.

While the Saigon regime of Ngo Dinh Diem soon disencumbered itself of Bao Dai and freed itself of French control, it failed to satisfy nationalist aspirations. Ho Chi Minh, who for the previous decade had been the acknowledged head of the Vietnamese nationalist movement, simply could not be displaced by Ngo Dinh Diem, a man supported from the outside, little known, and absent from the country during the critical years of the war against the French. Partition did not mean that the area south of the 17th parallel emerged free of Communist influence or of predispositions toward the regime of Ho Chi Minh. The population there could

[3] See Appendix I-C.

not forget that it was the Vietminh regime, now ensconced in the North, that drove out the French; and many landless peasants remembered that it was the Vietminh that had divided up the estates of absentee landlords for their benefit.

By helping to establish a separate state south of the armistice line, the United States was clearly acting in defiance of the Geneva Accords. In effect, both the United States and Saigon accepted, and insisted that Hanoi accept, only those aspects of the Geneva Agreements that they found advantageous and repudiated those provisions that they regarded as contrary to their interests. Thus, with American encouragement, Diem announced in mid-1955 that the elections promised at Geneva would not be held. Until 1958 the Hanoi government persisted in its efforts to arrange for the promised elections, but Diem, consistently backed by the United States, refused. During at least the first three years of the post-Geneva period, there was a lull in the military struggle. Hanoi refrained from support of insurrectionary activity in the South. But by repudiating the heart of the Geneva Agreements, Diem made civil war inevitable. When, in a civil war, a military struggle for power ends on the agreed condition that the competition will be transferred to the political level, the side which repudiates the agreed conditions must expect that the military struggle will be resumed.

Although American support was given to Diem, the United States did not make a blank-check commitment to whatever regime happened to hold power in Saigon. What has been referred to as "the U.S. commitment" was a limited, qualified pledge of economic support, and it was made specifically to Diem's government. It was not in any sense a pledge of *military* support. The cornerstone of our Vietnam involvement, President Eisenhower's letter to Diem in October 1954, was simply an undertaking "to examine" with Diem "how an intelligent program of American aid given directly to your government can assist Vietnam . . . in developing and maintaining a strong, viable state, capable of resisting attempted subversion or aggression through military means." A critical qualification was that even this economic aid was to be subject to Diem's carrying through reforms responsive to the aspirations of the Vietnamese people. Thus, in concluding his letter, President Eisenhower wrote:

The Government of the United States expects that this aid will be met by performance on the part of the Government of Vietnam in undertaking needed reforms. It hopes that such aid, combined with your own continuing efforts, will contribute effectively toward an independent Vietnam endowed with a strong government. Such a government would, I hope, be so responsive to the nationalist aspirations of its people, so enlightened in purpose and effective in performance, that it will be respected both at home and abroad and discourage any who might wish to impose a foreign ideology on your free people.

This is the substance of the Eisenhower commitment to which the present administration often refers when it is invoking American honor.

Except for Eisenhower's letter, the only other undertaking which the Administration cites as a proof of a Vietnam commitment is the treaty of the Southeast Asia Treaty Organization. But this treaty involves no American pledge to the South Vietnamese government, which was not and could not be a signatory. With respect to the *area* of South Vietnam, and also that of Cambodia and Laos, SEATO provides that in cases of aggression by armed attack, each SEATO power is "to meet the common danger in accordance with its constitutional processes," and in cases of subversion, to "consult" with the several SEATO signatories "in order to agree on the measures to be taken for common defense." SEATO, then, was not and is not a pledge to the government of South Vietnam. The treaty merely provides that each member country should determine whether its own security interests require it to respond to developments in that area and, when this happens, to consult with other signatories on any defense measure to be taken. The United States has certainly never been able to bring its SEATO allies to agree that the treaty's vague language could possibly be translated as any kind of commitment to the government of South Vietnam. President Kennedy's view of the United States commitment is best summed up in the statement he made in September 1963, when he said: "In the final analysis, it's their war. They're the ones who have to win it or lose it. We can help them, give them equipment, we can send our men out there as advisers but they have to win it."

Like those of Ho Chi Minh, the methods of Ngo Dinh Diem were authoritarian; but they were not administratively effective. Unlike Ho, Diem lacked contact with the bulk of his people, and he had no trained and dedicated party cadres and officials upon whom to rely. Most of the educated people who have worked in Diem's government and the governments that have succeeded it have been of two kinds: southerners who had collaborated with the French and thereby alienated the local population; or anti-Communist refugees from the North without roots in South Vietnam, men who speak a different dialect and most of whom are Roman Catholic, a religion foreign to the overwhelming majority of southerners. Moreover, at a very early stage Diem antagonized a large part of the southern peasantry by largely undoing the agrarian reforms that Ho Chi Minh's regime had carried out. Lands previously divided among the peasantry were restored to the landlords, and police supported the collection of five years' back rent. In mid-1956 Diem uprooted the traditional system of village autonomy by abolishing the elected village councils. He replaced them with officials who were appointed by and served as agents of the central government. Diem also removed many able and popular officials, leaders with strong local roots who had worked under the previous Vietminh administration. These men were often replaced with corrupt and oppressive appointees from outside, further alienating the rural population.

Diem governed with a harsh and heavy hand, countenancing no genuine opposition to his regime and indiscriminately denouncing as Communists those who opposed him, whatever their political views. By 1957 the harshness of Diem's repression had sparked uprisings against him, often not Communist-led. The Vietcong was able to build upon these later when its cadres became active. By 1958, former Vietminh supporters living in the South had begun to organize guerrilla operations against Diem, undertaking by 1959 a campaign of assassination of village chiefs. It must be recognized that this campaign, although often effective in disrupting Diem's efforts to establish his own administration throughout the country, did not antagonize the rural population so widely as some accounts have suggested. In fact, these assassinations were largely on a selective basis. The underground organization showed canny intelligence in eliminating the most unpopular Diem-appointed officials. Thus, the veteran Southeast Asian correspondent, Denis Warner, hardly a supporter of Hanoi, writes in his book, *The Last Confucian* (p. 89): "Summary Viet Cong justice for a village chief guilty of corruption or brutality did not offend the peasants. On the contrary, it tended to endow the Viet Cong with some of the characteristics of Robin Hood and his band of merry men . . ."

The exact point at which Hanoi began to support insurrectionary activity in the South is subject to much dispute, but certainly in 1960 such support was made public by Hanoi. In September of that year, Ho Chi Minh's government formally acknowledged the southern dissidents as the National Front for the Liberation of South Vietnam (NFLSV). This was in effect the political arm of the insurgents, a grouping that Diem collectively labeled "Vietcong" and that certainly incorporated a large number of the Vietminh's former adherents in the South as well as other elements opposed to Diem. The leader of the National Liberation Front, Nguyen Huu Tho, is a southerner, a Saigon lawyer first arrested during the period of French control and later, in November of 1954, by Diem. While still in jail, in 1959, he wrote a letter to ex-Vietminh southerners urging them to form a national front. In May 1961, approximately a year after the Front was formally established, he escaped from prison and soon emerged as the Front's principal leader. According to Tran Van Huu, who served as Bao Dai's prime minister from 1951 to 1953, Nguyen Huu Tho is "very well known in Saigon as a person who was most active in opposition to the French in the colonial period." By 1960 members of the Vietcong were being given training in the North, and some arms were being sent south, although the vast majority of the arms employed by the insurgents continued to be American equipment captured from or sold by Diem's troops.

Meanwhile, United States officials in Vietnam were increasingly frustrated in their efforts to induce Diem to institute the sort of reforms necessary for winning popular support. The hope that full and unstinting American backing would make him more cooperative in such matters proved totally illusory. Critically important social and economic reforms urged by the United States were either not carried out or were attended by so much corruption and inefficiency that they resulted in even greater alienation of the population. Diem's program of "agrarian reform" could hardly have been expected to secure him significant political support. Even the modest redistribution of land for which it provided did not get underway until 1958. The program was restricted to rice-growing lands; and even with regard to these holdings, landlords were permitted to keep up to 284 acres. Where rice properties in excess of this amount were made available for redistribution, the peasant had to pay for the land in full, and he received title to it only after he had paid the last of six installments. For those many landless peasants in the South who had been given such lands by the Vietminh in the period before Geneva, the right to purchase what they regarded as already their own did not make them particularly grateful to the government in Saigon. The strategic hamlet program, for which American officials initially made such extravagant claims, turned out to be in most areas a tragic failure that worked great hardship upon and further alienated the rural population. Its objective was to resettle peasants in larger and more easily protected concentrations where they were to benefit from new or improved social services. In fact, most of the peasantry affected were significantly worse off than before. Apart from the trauma of being uprooted from their homes and ancestral lands, they were usually quite inadequately compensated for the property they had been forced to abandon. They were often harshly treated, generally unable to discover the new social services they had been promised, and usually no better protected than before from the ravages of guerrilla warfare.

Despite repeated optimistic pronouncements by American military and civilian officials, by 1963 it had become clear to President Kennedy that Diem and his family were incapable of stemming the rapid political and military disintegration of the South Vietnamese regime. The massive build-up of American aid to the South Vietnamese army had proved ineffective, for the Vietcong benefited more from the vast infusion of American weapons than did the South Vietnamese army and had, in fact, been able to use the government as a supply store.

It was the highly publicized, heavy-handed treatment of South Vietnam's Buddhists that provided the Administration with the means of getting off the Diem hook in a way acceptable to members of Congress who might otherwise have attacked it with the charge of opposing an anti-Communist government. In effect, Washington signaled to the military in South Vietnam that we had abandoned our policy of "sink or swim with Diem" and would be pleased to see the army take over.

This was a calculated risk and a policy born of desperation. For there was no assurance that the Vietnamese army would be able to establish an effective government or command sufficient popular support. But it was believed that if the army were relieved of the constraints of Diem and his coterie, it would fight more effectively. This expectation, however, disregarded several facts. First, there was a lack of unity within the army. Second, the Vietcong had already built up its strength in the South and controlled over half the area. Third, even in that part of the country controlled by Diem, and particularly in the rural areas, the military leaders enjoyed little or no more support than did Diem. Thus, contrary to expectations, the army was no more successful than Diem, either in building popular support or in carrying out the measures necessary to secure such support. For a period of about three months following the overthrow of Diem, political controls were relaxed and the military junta headed by "Big Minh" (General Duong Van Minh) gave public opinion greater freedom of expression than it had probably ever enjoyed before. However, with the coup d'état of General Nguyen Khanh on January 30, 1964, the government returned to the level of repression that had existed under Diem, and the several governments installed by the subsquent series of coups have been only a little less or a little more repressive. The area of South Vietnam controlled by Saigon continued to shrink. By the end of 1964 a crisis was emerging, with Saigon's position being eroded at an accelerating rate, both politically and militarily. The deterioration of the military situation was reflected in a rate of desertion among new recruits that had increased to 30 per cent by January of 1965. The disintegrating position of the Saigon administration coincided with a perceptible growth in war-weariness among the South Vietnamese. Demands for a peaceful settlement multiplied. In Saigon itself, as well as in such Buddhist strongholds as Hué, students and monks publicly advocated an end to the fighting and called for negotiations with Hanoi.

It was at this juncture that the Johnson Administration, fearing that the Saigon army and government would fall apart, undertook to stiffen their morale with direct American military intervention and the bombing of North Vietnam. Increasing the direct American military involvement, to a point where the United States has assumed the major burden of offensive military operations against the Vietcong, has undoubtedly reduced the disposition of the South Vietnamese military leaders, and other members of that minority that has a vested interest in the present regime, to come to any negotiated settlement with the Vietcong. It is claimed that increased American involvement has had a similar effect on most of the civilian population, but such an effect is difficult to demonstrate because the present junta led by General Ky has outlawed as traitors all those who urge negotiations with the Vietcong or even discuss the possibility of a peaceful settlement.

The history of these two decades of increasing American involvement in Vietnam shows the danger of ignoring the underlying ground swell of nationalism with its strong accent on anti-colonialism. Having reviewed this history, perhaps we can understand why the school teacher in Hué said that the Americans are making Communists of the Vietnamese men. Starting from a wrong assumption, the United States has piled one error on another, moving deeper and deeper into a deteriorating situation. In the midst of a full-scale war, the choices are limited to desperate alternatives. Constructive solutions are hard to find. What has happened to the attempts to find a formula for negotiations? What kind of a settlement may be possible?

6:   The Negotiation Puzzle

In July 1965, it was brought to public notice,[1] and subsequently admitted by the United States Department of State, that in September 1964 the North Vietnamese government offered through U Thant to send a representative to Rangoon to meet with a United States representative and discuss the ending of hostilities in Vietnam. The United States did not reply to this offer for two months, presumably because of the presidential election, and then rejected it.

At that time the war was going badly for the United States and Secretary of Defense McNamara is reported to have felt that the shaky Saigon government could not survive the prospect of peace talks. The reason now officially given for the rejection is that Secretary of State Rusk's "antennae" did not indicate to him that the North Vietnamese seriously wanted to negotiate.[2] He apparently did not think it important to verify this by arranging the requested quiet discussions. Later U Thant tried for an outright cease-fire, offering to forward to the other side any terms the United States wished to propose even including the drawing of a truce line through Laos as well as Vietnam. Again he was rebuffed by the United States.

Though these facts came as a shock to most Americans and

[1] Eric Sevareid, CBS Radio, London, July 28, 1965, and *Look*, November 26, 1965.
[2] Robert McCloskey, *New York Times,* November 17, 1965.

created something of a crisis of confidence in the government, a careful reading of the *New York Times* shows that the United States has rejected no fewer than seven efforts to negotiate an end to the war.

As early as the fall of 1963, at a press conference right after Diem's assassination, Secretary Rusk turned down a French proposal for a neutral, independent South Vietnam.[3] Hanoi, at this time, expressed willingness to discuss the establishment of a coalition, neutralist government in South Vietnam.[4] In July 1964, the United States rejected a suggestion by U Thant for reconvening the Geneva Conference[5] of the nine nations that had negotiated the original settlement of the Indochina War in 1954. In December 1964, Ho Chi Minh notified France of his desire to discuss an accommodation with the United States; and in early February 1965, President de Gaulle, at the urging of North Vietnam, requested a reconvening of the Geneva Conference to discuss the future of Southeast Asia and the United Nations.[6] There were indications that the People's Republic of China would have been willing to attend and that withdrawal of United States forces from South Vietnam would not have been a prerequisite, provided eventual withdrawal could be expected as a result of a peace settlement. The Administration's reaction was to say that we had given France no mandate to act as a mediator and were not interested in a return to the conference table at that time. On February 24, the Soviet Union, angering some of the other Communist countries by doing so, joined France to press for reconvening the Geneva Conference to negotiate a settlement for South Vietnam.[7]

At this same time U Thant suggested possible preliminaries to a Geneva-type conference to discuss a possible peace settlement: interlinked dialogues[8] among the parties most directly involved, and an informal seven-power conference,[9] including all the Geneva

[3] Marcus Raskin and Bernard Fall, *Vietnam Reader* (New York: Random House, 1965).

[4] *New York Times,* March 9, 1965, and *Manchester Guardian,* August 9, 1965.

[5] *New York Times,* March 9, 1965.

[6] Drew Middleton, *New York Times,* February 23, 1965.

[7] Drew Middleton, *New York Times,* February 25, 1965.

[8] Thomas Hamilton, *New York Times,* February 25, 1965.

[9] Thomas Hamilton, *New York Times,* March 9, 1965.

powers except Laos and Cambodia. North Vietnam indicated itself receptive to this suggestion, as did France.[10] The United States, however, replied coldly, "There are no authorized negotiations under way with Mr. Thant or any other government." [11] U Thant further drew upon himself the wrath of the United States government by saying, "I am sure that the great American people, if only they knew the true facts and the background of the developments in Vietnam, will agree with me that further bloodshed is unnecessary." [12]

Hoping that the mere opening of negotiations might result in a tacit ceasefire, France urged that neither the United States nor the People's Republic of China make any preconditions to negotiations.[13] But Secretary Rusk said that the United States would agree to no conference until after North Vietnam had stopped the flow of men and arms to the Vietcong.[14] Furthermore, he refused to commit the Administration to any definite course, even if North Vietnam agreed to end its support of the Vietcong.[15] On February 27, the State Department published its widely disputed White Paper in an effort to prove that this support was preponderant.

In February and early March 1965 the United States was beginning large-scale American-piloted combat missions against the Vietcong in South Vietnam and massive air raids against North Vietnam. These were no longer retaliation against specific provocative acts but were an avowed effort to punish North Vietnam until officials were willing to negotiate on terms acceptable to the United States. At the same time, Secretary Rusk made it clear that the preconditions for any negotiations must be North Vietnam's cessation of all aid to the Vietcong and an assurance that the peace settlement would insure the "security and independence" of South Vietnam.[16] This was interpreted in Vietnam to mean

[10] New York Times, February 26, 1965.
[11] George E. Reedy, White House Press Secretary, as quoted by Max Frankel, New York Times, February 25, 1965.
[12] New York Times, February 25, 1965.
[13] New York Times, February 26, 1965.
[14] Max Frankel, New York Times, February 26, 1965.
[15] Drew Middleton, New York Times, February 25, 1965.
[16] New York Times, February 26, 1965.

that the United States intends to keep its military forces in South Vietnam indefinitely and that North Vietnam must abandon its goal of reunification of Vietnam. North Vietnam showed no interest in these terms and the National Liberation Front flatly rejected any attempts to negotiate as long as any United States forces remained in Vietnam.[17]

On April 1, however, William Warbey, a British Labor MP, reported that his talks with Ho Chi Minh indicated that the only precondition for negotiations on which the North would insist was cessation of United States bombing attacks upon it.[18]

On April 7, President Johnson, in his speech at Johns Hopkins University, declared that the United States would consent to "unconditional discussions." He stipulated, however, that the United States would settle for nothing less than an "independent" South Vietnam. His speech was predicated on the assumption that the National Liberation Front was an adversary with whom the United States was not willing to negotiate. He insisted that North Vietnam, urged on by Peking, was the aggressor, and that orders, men, supplies, and arms flowing in from the North were "the heartbeat of the war." This lent special significance to his proviso that the United States would enter into discussions with the *governments* concerned.

Reactions to this speech were predictable. The National Liberation Front considered the speech proof that the United States was ignoring it, the chief antagonist. The National Liberation Front and North Vietnam both knew that Hanoi could not end the war on behalf of the National Liberation Front, even if it wanted to do so. Peking rejected the speech as a device for perpetuating the partition of Vietnam and letting the United States stay on in South Vietnam, thus ensuring the rule of the American puppet government there.[19]

On April 11, the South Vietnamese government published a leaflet that was scattered by American planes over North Vietnam.[20] This leaflet stated that the National Liberation Front would

[17] *New York Times,* March 9, 1965.
[18] *The Times of London,* April 1, 1965.
[19] *New York Times,* April 9, 1965.
[20] From United States Information Agency, Saigon.

be barred from all negotiation, since it is "only an instrument created by the Communist North Vietnamese." The leaflet also declared that negotiations could take place only after "preconditions (such as the withdrawal of Communist troops and cadres) laid out by the Republic of Vietnam during eventual preliminary talks will have been accepted and carried out." This withdrawal was further specified as meaning "previous withdrawal of the Vietcong armed units and political cadres" as well as those of the North Vietnamese. This amounted to a denial of the President's offer of "unconditional" discussions.

A senior North Vietnamese diplomat announced that, since major North Vietnamese objectives are reunification and neutralization of Vietnam, withdrawal of United States forces and a coalition government in South Vietnam were essential to any settlement, and therefore negotiations on President Johnson's terms would amount to surrender.[21] On April 8, 1965, Premier Pham Van Dong of the Democratic Republic (North Vietnam) stated the Four Points, to be discussed below, as the basis on which it would agree to a Geneva-type conference for negotiating a peace settlement.

The National Liberation Front's negotiating position, which had hardened in March as soon as the first United States Marines landed in South Vietnam, was now matched by a hardening of North Vietnam's position as indicated by Hanoi's refusal to receive U Thant or, finally, even letters from him.[22] North Vietnam also refused to receive British missions to explore the possibility of negotiations. Even if the United States' negotiating position were to become clear and reasonably satisfactory to North Vietnam, Hanoi was not likely to agree to negotiate while United States bombings continued.

In mid-May, hard-pressed by critics at home and abroad, the United States halted its bombing of North Vietnam. It was later revealed [23] that Secretary of State Rusk transmitted a secret message to Hanoi at this time through the North Vietnamese Embassy in Moscow. The message stated that the bombing suspension could

[21] *New York Times,* April 10, 1965.
[22] Drew Middleton, *New York Times,* December 3, 1965.
[23] Editorial, *New York Times,* December 30, 1965.

be extended if there were "significant reductions" in Communist armed attacks in South Vietnam. "A permanent end" to the bombing in the North, it said, could only come through an end to armed attacks by the Vietcong in the South. There was no mention of negotiations or even informal discussions, such as President Johnson had proposed on April 7. There was no reference to Hanoi's "Four Points" peace plan of April 8, 1965. The bombings were resumed after five days, hardly enough time for the National Liberation Front and North Vietnam to consult on any proposal for negotiations. In spite of this short interval of time and the tone of the American note, which was close to an ultimatum, a response did come from Hanoi. The day before the bombings were resumed, the government of North Vietnam contacted the French government and asked it to inform Washington that North Vietnam was prepared to negotiate on the basis of its Four Points without demanding the prior complete withdrawal of United States forces from South Vietnam. High-ranking French officials, while admitting that this offer from Hanoi did not make any substantial concessions to the United States, expressed regret that even though, as the State Department contends, the offer was not transmitted to it until a few hours after the bombings had been resumed, the United States did not again halt the bombings long enough to induce a possible improvement in the offer.[24]

One cannot but be amazed, in view of these seven documented missed opportunities for exploring the sincerity of North Vietnamese offers for negotiation, that President Johnson declared at his press conference on July 13, "I must say that candor compels me to tell you that there has not been the slightest indication that the other side is interested in negotiation or in unconditional discussion, although the United States has made some dozen separate attempts to bring that about."

The experience in November and December 1965, regarding another apparent peace feeler, seems to emphasize the lessons of prior incidents. At the very time that Secretary of State Rusk was seeking clarification of a reported statement on negotiations by Ho Chi Minh, United States planes bombed a power plant only fourteen miles from Haiphong, opening up a new phase of escala-

[24] *New York Times,* November 19, 1965.

tion. Rusk's television interview at this time expressed the most rigid administration view with regard to the National Liberation Front.[25] The United States cannot expect to escalate the war of deeds and words and at the same time talk peace.[26]

What, exactly, are the points that have been set forth by the North Vietnamese, the National Liberation Front, and the United States as a basis for negotiation? Are they so far apart that there is no possible basis for discussion at a conference table? Let us first look at the various negotiating points, then consider developments that indicate a converging of views.

A. North Vietnam

The firmly repeated negotiating position of Hanoi was first given in the following statement of Premier Pham Van Dong on April 8, 1965.

It is the unswerving policy of the government of the D.R.V. [Democratic Republic of Vietnam] to strictly respect the 1954 Geneva Agreements on Viet-Nam and to correctly implement their basic provisions as embodied in the following points:

1. Recognition of the basic national rights of the Vietnamese people—peace, independence, sovereignty, unity and territorial integrity. According to the Geneva Agreements, the United States government must withdraw from South Viet-Nam United States troops, military personnel, and weapons of all kinds, dismantle all United States military bases there, cancel its "military alliance" with South Viet-Nam. It must end its policy of intervention and aggression in South Viet-Nam. According to the Geneva Agreements, the United States government must stop its acts of war against North Viet-Nam, completely cease all encroachments on the territory and sovereignty of the D.R.V.

2. Pending the peaceful reunification of Viet-Nam, while Viet-Nam is still temporarily divided into two zones, the military provisions of the 1954 Geneva Agreements on Viet-Nam must be strictly respected. The two zones must refrain from joining any military alliance with foreign countries. There must be no foreign military bases, troops, or military personnel in their respective territory.

3. The internal affairs of South Viet-Nam must be settled by the

[25] *New York Times,* December 8, 1965.
[26] See Arthur Krock, *New York Times,* December 21, 1965.

South Vietnamese people themselves, in accordance with the program of the NFLSV [the South Vietnam National Liberation Front], without any foreign interference.

4. The peaceful reunification of Viet-Nam is to be settled by the Vietnamese people in both zones, without any foreign interference.[27]

B. The National Liberation Front

The program of the National Liberation Front of South Vietnam referred to in the statement of Premier Pham Van Dong was issued on December 20, 1960. It consists of ten major headings with numerous subheadings dealing with the overthrow of the "camouflaged colonial regime of the American imperialists"; proposals for liberal democratic reform and civil rights; for economic improvement, agrarian reform, cultural and educational development, creation of a national army, a foreign policy of peace and neutrality, preparation for reunification, and the defense of universal peace. A few of the clauses most pertinent for this negotiation study are here excerpted:[28]

—Elect a new National Assembly through universal suffrage.
—Reward officers and soldiers having participated in the struggle against the domination by the Americans and their servants; adopt a policy of clemency toward the former collaborators of the Americans and Diemists guilty of crimes against the people but who have finally repented and are ready to serve the people.
—Abolish all foreign military bases established on the territory of Viet-Nam.
—Stay out of any military bloc; refuse any military alliance with another country.
—Accept economic aid from any country willing to help us without attaching any conditions to such help.
—The National Liberation Front of South Viet-Nam advocates the peaceful reunification by stages, on the basis of negotiation and through the seeking of ways and means in conformity with the interests of the Vietnamese nation.
—Commercial and cultural exchanges between the two zones will be implemented; the inhabitants of the two zones will be free to move

[27] Submitted in a government report from Hanoi dated April 1965, reported in *New York Times,* August 14, 1965.
[28] The full document is given in Appendix II.

about throughout the country. . . . The freedom of postal exchanges will be guaranteed.[29]

Statements of the National Liberation Front's negotiating position were given to an American professor, Robert S. Browne, and a French journalist, Georges Chaffard. These indicate considerable extension from the ten-point program which did not deal directly with negotiation or the Geneva accords.

Browne reports that the National Liberation Front calls for:

1. An immediate cease-fire, with a freezing of the current military position.
2. Adjudication by an international body in districts where control is in dispute.
3. United States preparation and execution of troop withdrawal over a six-month period.
4. A district-by-district election campaign from which a coalition government could emerge.[30]

Chaffard received a longer and more comprehensive statement from Huyn Tan Phat, the Vice-President of the National Liberation Front:

Our first task will be to rebuild the economy of South Vietnam. For that we will need . . . foreign economic aid and foreign investments. . . . To get aid from western countries we will have to follow a policy of neutrality. We know the capitalists. They will want guarantees. We are realists. Even United States aid will be welcome.

The unification of the armed forces and of the administration, the coexistence of cadres of diverse origins . . . this is going to present delicate problems. . . .

We shall be obliged to observe neutrality. How long will that last? Ten years? Fifteen? More perhaps. . . .

We will not even approach the problem of unification for a very long time. . . . One can see that the . . . structure . . . will differ more from the north. That will delay reunification. . . . When the time comes for unification it will take place on a basis precluding annexation of one zone by another.[31]

[29] Marcus G. Raskin, Bernard B. Fall, *The Viet-Nam Reader,* pp. 216-221.
[30] *New York Times,* July 22, 1965.
[31] *Viet Report,* July 1965, quoting *l'Expresse,* April 25, 1965.

C. United States

On August 3, 1965, Dean Rusk set forth the United States position on negotiating principles.

1. An end to aggression and subversion.
2. Freedom for South Vietnam to choose and shape for itself its own destiny, in conformity with democratic principles and without any foreign interference.
3. As soon as aggression has ceased, the ending of the military measures now necessary by the Government of South Vietnam and the nations that have come to its aid . . . and the removal of foreign military forces from South Vietnam.

We endorse these principles. In essence they constitute a return to the basic purpose of the Geneva accords of 1954. Further relations could be worked out by peaceful means. And this means the question of a free decision by the people of North and South Vietnam on the matter of reunification. . . . When the aggression has ceased and the freedom of South Vietnam is assured, we will withdraw our forces. . . . When the men and arms infiltrated by the north are withdrawn and Hanoi ceases its support and guidance of the war in the south, whatever remains in the form of indigenous dissent is a matter for the South Vietnamese themselves.[32]

A summary of the United States negotiating positions was recently given by Arthur J. Goldberg, United States Ambassador to the United Nations, in a letter to Secretary General U Thant in which he reported on the far-flung New Year efforts of the government to seek peace.

Among the points made in our messages conveyed to a number of governments are the following: that the United States is prepared for discussions or negotiations without any prior conditions whatsoever or on the basis of the Geneva accords of 1954 and 1962, that a reciprocal reduction of hostilities could be envisaged and that a cease-fire might be the first order of business in any discussions or negotiations, that the United States remains prepared to withdraw its forces from South Vietnam as soon as South Vietnam is in a position to determine its own future without external interference, that the United States desires no continuing military presence or bases in Viet-

[33] *Why Vietnam* (Government Printing Office, Washington, D.C., 1965).

nam, that the future political structure in South Vietnam should be determined by the South Vietnamese people themselves through democratic processes and that the question of the reunification of the two Vietnams should be decided by the free decision of their two peoples.[33]

A close scrutiny of the points above reveals that starting from mutually incompatible and apparently rigid negotiating positions in the winter of 1964-65—each demanding from the other the equivalent of unconditional surrender—certain aspects of the negotiating positions of both sides became more flexible and their peace terms seemed to be converging significantly.

1. *Geneva Agreements.* Both sides claim that they want to negotiate on the basis of the 1954 Geneva Agreements, although North Vietnam emphasizes that this means United States withdrawal and conducting the elections which the United States blocked in 1956; whereas the United States has tended to emphasize that it means (1) North Vietnamese withdrawal, (2) acceptance of the political partition of Vietnam, authorized only as a temporary military division in 1954, and (3) the acceptance by the National Liberation Front of political conditions before it came into existence.

2. *Hanoi's Four Points and United States Withdrawal.* The United States has moved from adamant rejection of Hanoi's Four Points when they were put forth in April to an avowed willingness to discuss them as part of the agenda for negotiations. A crucial point is the question of withdrawal of American military forces. This is put as the first of the Four Points, and in every public utterance from Hanoi it is the implied basis upon which any negotiations must be started. There have been repeated hints, however, from North Vietnamese and National Liberation Front officials in Algiers,[34] Prague,[35] Paris,[36] and Moscow[37] that the withdrawal of United States forces from South Vietnam may not be a precondition for starting negotiations as long as withdrawal is understood to be a necessary result of a peace settlement. This was also

[33] United States Mission to the United Nations, Press Release No. 4781, January 5, 1966.

[34] Sanford Gottlieb, *Sane World,* September 1965.

[35] *New York Times,* October 28, 1965.

[36] Sanford Gottlieb, *Sane World,* September 1965.

[37] Lord Fenner Brockway, *New York Times,* August 22, 1965.

the message of Mr. Janos Peter, Foreign Minister of Hungary, in his message to the United Nations General Assembly in October 1965. Meanwhile, the United States has declared that all it wants is a settlement that will permit its honorable withdrawal from Vietnam.

3. *Autonomy of South Vietnam and Reunification.* Point four of the Hanoi pronouncement indicates considerable modification of the Geneva accord which provided only a temporary military dividing line at the 17th parallel. North Vietnam has indicated its willingness to accept an autonomous regime in South Vietnam provided it "genuinely represents all major sections of the southern population" and that both governments should have the right to "enjoy economic, cultural, and fraternal relations" with countries of their own choice.[38] This represents a deference to the wishes of the National Liberation Front, which has indicated that it wants to delay reunification until it is strong and stable enough to negotiate with the North on terms of equality. The United States, while continually emphasizing a "free, independent South Vietnam," has nevertheless indicated acceptance of the right of North and South to unite, if they choose, without foreign interference.

4. *Third Party Presence.* The United States has moved from irritated outbursts over U Thant's efforts for negotiation to a general appeal to the United Nations to use its good offices[39] (though the United States has not formally laid the Vietnam problem before the United Nations as it was bound by the U.N. Charter to do before taking unilateral military action). The North Vietnamese have given some evidence that they accept the need of a third-party presence to supervise a cease-fire[40] and elections in South Vietnam, as specified by the Geneva Agreements of 1954. A question remains as to what kind of third party would be accepted by all parties and what the terms of reference would be. This would of necessity be a major part of negotiating discussions.

[38] William Warbey reporting interviews with Ho Chi Minh and Prime Minister Pham Van Dong in letter to the *Times of London,* April 1, 1965.
[39] See Ambassador Goldberg's letter to U Thant, *New York Times,* January 6, 1966.
[40] Fenner Brockway, *London Tribune,* September 10, 1965.

5. *The Place of the National Liberation Front and the Question of Elections.* The United States has moved from a position of refusal to recognize any right of the National Liberation Front to be at the negotiating table to a statement by President Johnson that the presence of the National Liberation Front is not an "insurmountable obstacle" and that they "would have no difficulty being represented and having their view represented." [41] The National Liberation Front and Hanoi, on the other hand, have insisted all along that the Front must have an independent role of its own in negotiations. Any hope deriving from the ambiguity of the President's statement was probably dashed by the statement of the Secretary of State in a television interview in December 1965. The *New York Times* reports that "Mr. Rusk indicated that the Vietcong's political organization, the National Liberation Front, would not be given any political status or influence in South Vietnam through negotiations." [42]

A question also remains about what type of South Vietnamese representative the National Liberation Front and the North Vietnamese will accept at the conference table. Public statements have indicated their unwillingness to treat with the Saigon government of General Ky.

The program of the National Liberation Front is Premier Pham Van Dong's third point. This has never been accepted by the United States. One part of the program is the election of a new widely representative National Assembly through universal suffrage.

The United States has indicated its willingness that free elections take place, but it has never stated that it would accept the inevitable election of National Liberation Front representatives, including some Communists, in the resulting South Vietnamese government. In fact, Secretary Rusk has said:

If the South Vietnamese people have a chance in free elections to make their own choices, they will not elect a Communist to power in Saigon. I do not believe that the South Vietnamese people will be the first people in history freely to elect a Communist regime.[43]

[41] President Johnson's press conference, July 28, 1965.
[42] Max Frankel, *New York Times,* December 8, 1965.
[43] Max Frankel, *New York Times,* December 8, 1965.

The Secretary of State may not intend this to mean that an election that chooses Communists is *ipso facto* not a free election, but to the Vietnamese citizen this must sound like the usual situation under the Diem regime in which lists of voters were drawn to rule out all dissident elements. Because of its political repercussions here in the United States, the proposal of any coalition government including Communists is a principal stumbling block for negotiations.

The course of negotiation feelers has gone through several phases. It is clear that the United States showed a complete coolness toward negotiations from the fall of the Diem regime on November 1, 1963, up to the President's Johns Hopkins speech on April 7, 1965. From that speech through the July 28 press conference and up to the events of the turn of the year, various expressions were made indicating an interest in negotiations, and separate elements of possible settlement were put forth. The sincerity of American offers was subject to question on four counts. First, any actual overtures from the other side were ignored or rebuffed as in the incident at the end of the five-day bombing lull in May. Second, the government in Saigon made frequent statements against negotiations and passed a law in May 1965 that made talk of peace a treasonable offense.[44] Third, each major statement for negotiations was coupled with the announcement of a new phase of armed forces build-up and offensive action. Fourth, there was no attempt on the part of the United States to put all its pieces of negotiation into one package and present it with conviction and corresponding action.

By the end of 1965 the cycle had run its complete course, and the Johnson Administration, rather than being aloof from any talk of negotiation, set forth on a dramatic worldwide effort to persuade all nations including Hanoi that the United States really wanted to bring the dispute from the battlefield to the conference table. Ambassador Harriman went to Poland, Yugoslavia, and India. (Poland and India are members of the International Control Commission for Vietnam; Yugoslavia is one of the nonaligned countries that has offered to mediate.) McGeorge Bundy, Special

[44] See Appendix III.

Assistant to the President, flew to Ottawa. (Canada is the third member of the Control Commission.) Arthur Goldberg, United States Ambassador to the United Nations, visited Pope Paul VI and then had high-level talks in Rome, Paris, and London. Vice-President Hubert Humphrey made a tour to the Far East to discuss Vietnam, among other things. Ambassador Kohler conferred with Soviet officials in Moscow. Assistant Secretary of State G. Mennen Williams explained Washington's position to the leaders of several African countries, and Under Secretary of State Thomas C. Mann did the same in Mexico City. This rather startling switch from secrecy to glaring publicity, from carefully controlled channels to "jet-diplomacy," as James Reston called it, brought forth no concessions from Hanoi and only more denunciations of a "peace-hoax."

The intensive peace efforts of those days may indicate that the President was genuinely interested in stopping the war, but the methods and the terms were not likely to be acceptable to the other side. As Ambassador Charles E. Bohlen has said, "In dealing with the Communists, remember that in their mind what is secret is serious, and what is public is merely propaganda." [45] A similar assessment is usually made in Washington concerning Communist approaches. The main ingredient lacking in the American peace recipe was any assurance that the National Liberation Front could have its own representative in the peace conference or in the future political arrangements for South Vietnam. The continued bombing in the South during the cessation of bombing in the North made it difficult for Hanoi to make offers without seeming to betray its ally in the South. Moreover, new units of troops were landed in South Vietnam, bringing the total to 190,000 at the end of the year, and the bombing of supply routes in Laos was greatly intensified.[46] Neither of these developments was likely to be regarded by Hanoi as an indication of peaceful intent or as a contribution to an atmosphere of negotiation.

This experience of the "peace offensive" of the 1966 New Year period brought into relief the false premises and mistaken assumptions that have shaped United States public opinion and

[45] Quoted by James Reston, *New York Times,* January 2, 1966.
[46] *New York Times,* January 8, 1966.

policy toward Vietnam and much of Southeast Asia for years. These misleading guidelines are recapitulated here as keys for understanding the negotiation puzzle and the kind of proposals that might bring a settlement. The first such false premise is that this "dirty little war" can be won. Policy makers in the United States seem to think that the National Liberation Front and North Vietnam can be bombed, burned, or starved into submission and that then a settlement advantageous to the United States and the forces it is backing can be reached. But this is to misread the special nature and the thirty-year history of the Communist-nationalist movement in Vietnam. The National Liberation Front and the North Vietnamese are fired with crusading zeal. Their determination to resist United States intrusion renders victory impossible in any complete sense. Thus far every escalation on the part of the United States has led to a corresponding effort by the Vietnamese nationalists and Communists, backed by increasing commitments from the Soviet Union and China.

The second unrealistic premise is that this is a war of aggression by the North Vietnamese instigated by China against the South. Such a view distorts the origin of the conflict, the role of the National Liberation Front, and the actual relationship between Hanoi and Peking. This is essentially a civil war. True, the National Liberation Front receives increasing support from the North Vietnamese, but the revolt in South Vietnam was begun and is still sustained by groups of South Vietnamese who turned against the Saigon government. Resistance against the Saigon government is likely to continue, gaining much propaganda advantage from the U.S. military operation. There is no reason to believe that the National Liberation Front will disappear from the scene. It is probably now the strongest indigenous political force in South Vietnam. Peking is offering support for what it considers a movement of liberation, but it is clear that the support thus far has not had a significant effect on the course of the conflict.

False premise number three is the assumption that if Vietnam becomes a Communist state, all the other countries in Southeast Asia will follow "like a row of dominoes." Vietnam is the setting for a unique convergence of nationalism and Communism. What happens there will not necessarily determine developments in other countries. Even if some countries should turn to Communism in their own socioeconomic revolutions, this need not threaten legitimate American interests. The United States has found it possible to get along with the Communist countries in eastern Europe and thus could presumably coexist with Communist countries in Southeast Asia. What the United States wants to avoid is the formation of strong hostile states, particularly such states dependent upon and aligned with China. But this is precisely what our present military policy promotes by preventing the natural development of national socioeconomic revolutions and forcing countries such as North Vietnam into dependence on China.

The fourth false premise is that if the United States reneges on its commitment to the Saigon regime, American credibility will be questioned in Europe as well as in Asia. This argument is the one most often raised in defense of United States policy. It seems to strike at the very heart of our honor as a nation. But what does this commitment actually mean? All-out commitment to the present Saigon government actually did not exist prior to the Johnson Administration. It was made by that Administration, albeit in terms suggesting that it was merely a logical continuation of earlier commitments made by Presidents Eisenhower and Kennedy. Now the Administration insists that an unlimited American commitment exists and that, this being so, the credibility of the American government is at stake in any settlement in Vietnam. Thus, although there are grounds for doubting the Administration's credibility in dealing candidly with the American people over the problem of Vietnam, the public is asked to give unreserved support to the government so that its credibility abroad will remain untarnished.

The Administration is actually trying to make credible what is not credible. It is not credible that American military power could be translated into political solutions where politically requisite conditions do not exist. It is not credible that confidence could be inspired among other countries by unflagging military pursuit of ends, even when these are unreal and inconsistent with basic political and social facts. It destroys both confidence and credibility when America pursues a mistaken course doggedly, regardless of the consequences, and regardless of the human suffering we inflict.

To give unqualified, undiscriminating support to a military junta, as during 1964 and 1965, only makes credible to the world the accusation that the United States has abandoned and violated the very political and ethical values upon which the country was founded.

American military power is credible. An Asian ambassador, interviewed in the summer of 1965, was asked whether a cessation of bombing by the United States would be interpreted as a sign of weakness. He replied:

Weakness!! With the 7th Fleet and the U.S. Air Force? All Asia—all the world—knows the United States is the most powerful nation in history, and can do what it wants. You don't have to show us that. We know it, and we don't understand how you can think that anyone will question your power.[47]

It is not the military credibility of the United States that is lacking, but credibility in matters of rationality, political maturity, and legal and moral responsibility. In the eyes of a large part of the world, United States conduct in Vietnam has already brought its credibility with respect to these nonmilitary qualities into question. Much can be done to restore American credibility and honor if the United States will abandon its clearly calamitous policy of reliance upon military means to achieve impossible political ends.

With policies built on such premises, it is understandable how the United States can be moving inexorably down the road of no return. But this is not the only path open. The *politically relevant* alternatives now facing the Administration are to continue escalating the war or to start de-escalating immediately and, in accordance with political realities, to make an effort to negotiate a cease-fire and a political settlement calling for the orderly withdrawal of United States military forces. The authors of this report now address themselves to exploring possible measures toward such a solution.

[47] Interview by Stephen G. Cary, AFSC staff member.

7: Possibilities for a Settlement

A political settlement with orderly withdrawal of American and allied military forces will not be easy to arrange. It is a course set with emotional booby traps and logical ambushes. The horror of the alternative makes us persevere in making proposals, no matter how tentative or easily betrayed by the next headline.

No solution in Vietnam is possible without a clear and unequivocal pronouncement by the United States that it intends to end the war with a settlement that will include withdrawing its forces and dismantling its military bases. This pronouncement will have to be supported by immediate and meaningful actions to prove our good faith. Until such intentions are made clear, neither the Saigon regime nor the National Liberation Front and Hanoi will take seriously any overtures on our part to negotiate. This will be especially true of governments in Saigon, such as that headed by Premier Ky which has consistently avoided any positive endorsement of negotiations right up through the 1966 New Year peace offensive,[1] even while the United States was indicating to the whole world its willingness to negotiate. The North Vietnamese are extremely suspicious of American intentions because, so often in the past, talk of our willingness to negotiate has been accompanied or followed by increased military efforts and because the bases the United States is now building at Cam Ranh Bay, Nha Trang,

[1] *New York Times,* January 16, 1966: Report of interview of Secretary Rusk and Premier Ky.

68

and Da Nang appear to them to be of a larger and more permanent kind than required by the present war in Vietnam. It is important, therefore, that while we ask for negotiations we also announce immediate steps of de-escalation such as the cessation of bombing in both North and South and a freeze on further troop build-up. Further steps could include refraining from provocative tactics such as patrols in force, unprovoked attacks, and efforts to expand the areas of occupation.

Any pronouncement by the United States must also affirm that the future of Vietnam should be decided by the Vietnamese themselves. At the same time, the United States should make clear that it is willing to sign and support such agreements as may be developed guaranteeing a settlement. This assurance could erase doubts stemming from the refusal of the United States to endorse the 1954 Geneva Accords. Pham Van Dong, premier of North Vietnam, has insisted on the importance of full United States participation in any agreement.[2] The pronouncement should make clear that the National Liberation Front would be included in any negotiations and in any political settlement in South Vietnam as a party in its own right and not an appendage of the Hanoi delegation. Such a declaration would probably open the way for desirable changes in the present political situation in Saigon. No one can foretell what might emerge in terms of local political forces. But it is possible that the nonmilitary elements that paved the way for the overthrow of the Diem regime and that have since been suppressed would re-emerge and could help speed the process of reaching a settlement.

Two unilateral steps then constitute the *sine qua non* for negotiations. Variants as to order of announcement or extent of action may be necessary; but before any serious negotiating is possible, the United States needs to make clear first that it does not plan to continue its military involvement and is starting on immediate steps of de-escalation and, second, that the Vietnamese, including the National Liberation Front, must decide their own fate. It is often said that by making unilateral moves the United States is giving up bargaining counters or even "blue chips" as if the Vietnamese situation were part of a complicated game. Our goal,

---

[2] William Warbey, MP, *New York Times*, November 28, 1965.

however, must be to bring the war to an end. Steps to convince our adversaries of our sincerity are evidently necessary.

While these initiatives are in progress, a whole series of forces, international to local, need to be brought to bear on the problems. The following progression is set forth, not as a rigid pattern, but as suggestive of the wide possibilities.

1. The United States could call for a general cease-fire for all parties, supervised by an international body to keep order and prevent reprisals. Such supervision might be carried on by the International Control Commission (ICC), which was set up by the Geneva Agreements and is composed of representatives of Canada, India, and Poland. The ICC would have to be enlarged or reorganized and given a firmer mandate in order to meet the objections on both sides to its present composition and functioning.

2. At the same time, a Geneva-type conference should be called together to reapply the principles of the Geneva Agreements of 1954 to the current situation. The logical group to form such a conference would be the original Geneva powers, which could be assembled on request from concerned parties by the co-chairmen, Britain and the Soviet Union. Some difficulties would arise in reconvening this group as originally constituted. For example, the National Liberation Front, which had no place in the framework of the original body, must be included now.

A more complicated problem is the official representation for the present Republic of Vietnam, or South Vietnam. The present military hierarchy in Saigon can be expected to do all in its power to resist efforts to end the war on terms it would regard as unfavorable. Its suppression of any expressions in favor of a peaceful settlement has made open organized opposition to the war impossible.[3] There is a large non-Communist sector of the population, of which the Buddhists and intellectual communities represent only a part, which is vitally interested in ending the war. Some means must be found to permit them to express themselves. This will require an end to censorship of the press, restored freedom for political discussion and organization, and the institution of some officially recognized body for public representation.

[3] See Appendix III: Decree Law outlawing Communism and pro-Communist neutralism.

One suggestion for achieving this is that the current Saigon government be pressed to establish a council of notables representing a wide cross section of civilian and religious leaders who, in conjunction with the Saigon government, could form a negotiating authority. Such a council might initiate a representative referendum in Saigon and other urban centers on the issue of whether or not the government should enter into negotiations with the National Liberation Front. Such a referendum might be conducted under international auspices, thus providing a precedent for the elections that will have to be conducted after a treaty is negotiated. Even then it would be difficult to arrange a fair vote because of unsettled political conditions, intensified by the large number of displaced persons.

If major obstacles arose in setting up a new Geneva-type conference, it might be necessary to convene a new group of concerned powers, possibly through the good offices of the United Nations Secretary General. Some exploratory efforts, preferably quiet and private, would clearly be necessary before a decision on the best way to solve this problem could be made.

The United Nations itself would in normal circumstances be the natural springboard for the launching of negotiations, the overseeing of a cease-fire, the policing of elections, and the carrying on of necessary peace-keeping activities. Expertise in these areas has been developed through years of varied experience. Many persons in the United States have suggested a major role for the United Nations. Unfortunately, in this case the United Nations faces the particular difficulty that it is not acceptable as a mediating body to the Democratic Republic of Vietnam, to the National Liberation Front, or to the People's Republic of China. Neither Hanoi nor Peking belongs to the United Nations. Ever since the Korean War they have viewed the world organization with great suspicion as a tool of the United States. In his policy declaration giving the Four Points, Premier Pham Van Dong said, "Any approach tending to secure a United Nations intervention in the Viet-Nam situation is also inappropriate because such approaches are basically at variance with the 1954 Geneva Agreements on Viet-Nam." The United States in its conduct has done little to allay this suspicion, and indeed in the midst of the whole escalation-negotiation see-saw in the fall of 1965, the State Department was engaged in convincing as many national representatives as possible that the government of mainland China should not be given the credentials for representing China in the United Nations. U Thant as Secretary General has made some helpful offers to mediate and he may yet play a valuable role.

3. Once the Geneva-type conference has been convened, its first task would be to encourage Saigon and the National Liberation Front to reach agreement on the formation of a Vietnamese Provisional Executive to maintain temporary administration of South Vietnam and take measures necessary for the establishment of a provisional government. Such arrangements would not be simple and the early inclusion of an international force is likely to be required. In an inflammatory situation with anarchy and chaos near the surface, transitional steps of government are not easily carried out. However, the experience of Algeria and the Dominican Republic can be cited to show that, at least under some circumstances, a provisional executive has been a possible formula.

4. International supervisory forces should be brought into South Vietnam under the aegis of the negotiating conference as early as possible. A natural starting point is the International Control Commission (ICC) set up for the Geneva Conference of 1954. Both sides have indicated willingness to use the ICC as a point of departure. Insofar as the provisional government can establish stable authority, the function of the international forces could be minimized, and yet they might be needed to restrain certain militant elements on either side which might attempt to sabotage the negotiations. Such a presence might also be of help in guaranteeing against reprisals.

5. The phased withdrawal of United States forces cannot be blueprinted this far in advance of negotiations. It is likely that as the provisional government, with the help of international police, takes over control, the United States forces should be withdrawn as rapidly as possible into three or four enclaves. These enclaves could be sanctuaries for refugees fearing reprisals and bases for logistical support that might still be needed for international forces. The drawing into enclaves would be a temporary move preparatory to complete withdrawal and dismantling of bases.

6. The provisional government would direct the demobilization of armed forces on both sides and the withdrawal from South Vietnam of all outside forces, both North Vietnamese and American, under the surveillance of the international presence. The provisional government would also be responsible for conducting elections, again under the scrutiny of an international umpire. The object of such elections might be a Constitutional Assembly or an actual permanent government.

7. Successful negotiations may still leave some elements in South Vietnam in danger of reprisals. Predictions have varied greatly as to the number of persons on either side who might need to seek sanctuary. The type of regime developed in negotiations and elections would make an important difference. On the side of optimistic predictions is the amazingly favorable experience of the amnesty and exchange of persons between the two zones after the first Geneva Conference. On the pessimistic side is the cruel nature of the current civil war, which may lead to personal vendettas in the villages and mass reprisals. The United States would certainly owe an obligation to assist persons who felt they might be in jeopardy because of the United States military withdrawal. A precedent is already at hand in the case of Cuban refugees. Special legislation would be needed to bring them into this country. This would be costly, but the war is now being conducted at an infinitely greater expense.

8. The final act of the Geneva-type conference should be an international agreement guaranteeing Vietnam's neutrality and its freedom from any outside interference. Major questions such as reunification should be left to the Vietnamese after the establishment of responsible government in South Vietnam and the achievement of relative stability. There should be guarantees against armed intervention or infiltration from either North or South Vietnam in the affairs of the other state, but it should be made clear that nothing in the agreement precludes eventual reunification of North and South should the Vietnamese so decide. Provisions for commercial and cultural exchange, freedom of movement, and postal service between the two countries might well be included.

9. The way may then be open to fulfill the long-delayed prom-

ises of massive economic aid to the people of Vietnam. In his April 7 speech President Johnson said:

> These countries of Southeast Asia are homes for millions of impoverished people. Each day these people rise at dawn and struggle through until the night to wrestle existence from the soil. They are often wracked by diseases, plagued by hunger, and death comes at the early age of 40. . . .
>
> The United Nations is already actively engaged in development in this area. . . . And I hope tonight that the Secretary General of the United Nations could use the prestige of his great office and his deep knowledge of Asia to initiate, as soon as possible, with the countries of that area, a plan for co-operation in increased development.
>
> For our part I will ask the Congress to join in a billion-dollar American investment in this effort as soon as it is under way.

To the indigenous problem of poverty has now been added the fantastic destruction of modern war. The American people have a responsibility to assist in the repair of the damage wrought to both South and North Vietnam by the war. It is imperative that we do so if we are to keep this area from becoming an explosive center for bitter anti-Americanism in the future. This will require vast amounts of United States aid, but will be far less costly than the continuation of the war. More important than the quantity of aid offered is the spirit in which it is offered. Any future part that the Americans play will require a high degree of respect for the people of Vietnam. Aid must be openly extended without strings attached. This is easier to do if it comes under the auspices of an international body. In general the United States will have to seek means to facilitate the economic and social revolution in the entire area, not as part of a tactic to "stop Communism" but as part of a positive program of dealing with the pressing needs of the people.

Full advantage should be taken of the cooperation already achieved by the United Nations Economic Commission for Asia and the Far East. Under its auspices plans for the Mekong River development have been laid, projecting a technological revolution affecting the lives of over 30 million people. The Asian Development Bank, soon to be in operation, with one billion dollars in resources, could be given a larger role. The Asian Institute for

Economic Development and Planning could greatly expand its efforts to train government officials. Following the example of the United Nations response to the Congo crisis, a special emergency reconstruction fund could be established under the United Nations which would mobilize the skill and experience available through other international agencies.

10. In every effort to achieve a settlement, the long-range goal of stability in Southeast Asia must be kept in mind. The United Nations could assist this process if both the People's Republic of China and the Democratic Republic of North Vietnam are no longer outlaws but participants in the world community of nations. This would require that the issue of Chinese representation in the U.N. be solved. North Vietnam, like South Vietnam, could then become an Observer at the U.N. with full opportunities to take part in the economic and social programs of the U.N. system and with opportunities for diplomatic consultation at Headquarters. With Peking as a member, and with some agreement reached for self-determination in the whole area of Vietnam, steps could be taken for some type of U.N. guarantee of the neutrality of Cambodia, Laos, and Vietnam. Underlying the immediate steps would be the broader objectives: the achievement of universality of membership in the U.N. and the development of accepted processes for the achievement of security through peaceful settlement, peaceful change, and the promotion of human rights.

Conclusion

As 1966 begins, hopes for a new day in Vietnam hang in the balance. Will the record of escalating horror in 1965 be extended in 1966, or will it be succeeded by a record of escalating peace? The past year of devastation and deadlock has shown the self-defeating nature of military solutions to political and economic problems. A new approach must be found.

The experience of Vietnam has shown the need for American understanding of the social forces impelling change in vast areas of the world. Our future and that of Asia, Africa, and Latin America are clearly interlocked. Although most Americans benefit from our growing productivity, the gap between the "have" and "have-not" peoples steadily widens. In their affluence, Americans can scarcely realize the desperation of peoples in most developing nations today. The ghettos of our own cities provide but a small sample of the social dynamite among the poorer nations. These conditions cannot be met by dogmatic anti-Communism. Revolutionary change of some kind is necessary. The tragedy of Vietnam shows that revolutionary forces can turn to civil war, and civil war can lead to outside intervention, and intervention can lead to an ever-widening arena of conflict, with the specter of the H-bomb looming as the ultimate debacle—all this unless the forces of change are channeled into constructive courses.

American understanding must go beyond turning from destructive to constructive approaches. It must become aware of the

76

subtle and dangerous assumption that the United States can determine the course of the whole world, either through military power or economic power. We condemn the concept of policing the world only to fall into the trap of trying to buy the world's allegiance with our largesse. The fallacy of the *Pax Americana* is still conditioning our thinking.

In the not-so-remote day when we were not a great power and were still looked down upon by the European powers, which were then engaged in exploiting Asia and Africa and parcelling out among themselves extraterritorial rights in China, America was admired everywhere. Refugees sought our shores. Patriots took inspiration and courage from the Declaration of Independence and the writings of Jefferson and Lincoln.

Now we are technically developed, rich, mighty—and no longer admired. The downtrodden multitudes look elsewhere, to the very elements that we are bent on destroying. We must refurbish the American dream and seek ways to enlarge it into a world dream. But we must remember that we Americans are only a small portion of the dreamers.

The world to come must be built on international accommodation and cooperation. The year 1965, when violence reached a new peak in Vietnam and the United Nations was crippled for nine months, was supposed to be International Cooperation Year. The new order struggles to be born against great difficulties. Progress in conquering disease leads to a setback in conquering poverty. The stresses of change produce strains within each new nation, and lead to heightened tensions between nations.

Americans have a natural optimism born of our experience, a faith that every condition of man can be changed for the better. If we can apply this faith with perspective and with understanding of those whose experience has been less fortunate, we will be able to share in building a world ruled by human rights and human dignity.

Appendix I: The 1954 Geneva Agreements on Vietnam

Appendix 1–A

(The Geneva Agreements theoretically ended the war between French Union forces and the Vietminh in Laos, Cambodia, and Vietnam. These states were to become fully independent countries, with the last-named partitioned near the 17th parallel into two states pending reunification through "free elections" to be held by July 20, 1956. The United States and Vietnam are not signatories to these agreements.)

Agreement on the Cessation of Hostilities in Viet-Nam, July 20, 1954

Chapter I—Provisional Military Demarcation Line and Demilitarized Zone

Article 1

A provisional military demarcation line shall be fixed, on either side of which the forces of the two parties shall be regrouped after their withdrawal, the forces of the People's Army of Viet-Nam to the north of the line and the forces of the French Union to the south.

The provisional military demarcation line is fixed as shown on the map attached [omitted].

It is also agreed that a demilitarized zone shall be established on either side of the demarcation line, to a width of not more than 5 kms. from it, to act as a buffer zone and avoid any incidents which might result in the resumption of hostilities.

Article 2

The period within which the movement of all the forces of either party into its regrouping zone on either side of the provisional military demarcation line shall be completed shall not exceed three hundred (300) days from the date of the present Agreement's entry into force.

Article 3

When the provisional military demarcation line coincides with a waterway, the waters of such waterway shall be open to civil navigation by both parties wherever one bank is controlled by one party and the other bank by the other party. The Joint Commission shall establish rules of navigation for the stretch of waterway in question. The merchant shipping and other civilian craft of each party shall have unrestricted access to the land under its military control.

Article 4

The provisional military demarcation line between the two final regrouping zones is extended into the territorial waters by a line perpendicular to the general line of the coast.

All coastal islands north of this boundary shall be evacuated by the armed forces of the French Union, and all islands south of it shall be evacuated by the forces of the People's Army of Viet-Nam.

Article 5

To avoid any incidents which might result in the resumption of hostilities, all military forces, supplies and equipment shall be withdrawn from the demilitarized zone within twenty-five (25) days of the present Agreement's entry into force.

Article 6

No person, military or civilian, shall be permitted to cross the provisional military demarcation line unless specifically authorized to do so by the Joint Commission.

Article 7

No person, military or civilian, shall be permitted to enter the demilitarized zone except persons concerned with the conduct of civil administration and relief and persons specifically authorized to enter by the Joint Commission.

Article 8

Civil administration and relief in the demilitarized zone on either side of the provisional military demarcation line shall be the responsibility of the Commanders-in-Chief of the two parties in their respective zones. The number of persons, military or civilian, from each side who are permitted to enter the demilitarized zone for the conduct of civil administration and relief shall be determined by the respective Commanders, but in no case shall the total number authorized by either side exceed at any one time a figure to be determined by the Trung Gia Military Commission or by the Joint Commission. The number of civil police and the arms to be carried by them shall be determined by the Joint Commission. No one else shall carry arms unless specifically authorized to do so by the Joint Commission.

Article 9

Nothing contained in this chapter shall be construed as limiting the complete freedom of movement, into, out of or within the demilitarized zone, of the Joint Commission, its joint groups, the International Commission to be set up as indicated below, its inspection teams and any other persons, supplies or equipment specifically authorized to enter the demilitarized zone by the Joint Commission. Freedom of movement shall be permitted across the territory under the military control of either side over any road or waterway which has to be taken between points within the demilitarized zone when such points are not connected by roads or waterways lying completely within the demilitarized zone.

Chapter II—Principles and Procedure Governing
Implementation of the Present Agreement

Article 10

The Commanders of the Forces on each side, on the one side the
Commander-in-Chief of the French Union forces in Indo-China and
on the other side the Commander-in-Chief of the People's Army of
Viet-Nam, shall order and enforce the complete cessation of all hostilities in Viet-Nam by all armed forces under their control, including all
units and personnel of the ground, naval, and air forces.

Article 11

In accordance with the principle of a simultaneous cease-fire
throughout Indo-China, the cessation of hostilities shall be simultaneous throughout all parts of Viet-Nam, in all areas of hostilities and
for all the forces of the two parties.

Taking into account the time effectively required to transmit the
cease-fire order down to the lowest echelons of the combatant forces
on both sides, the two parties are agreed that the cease-fire shall take
effect completely and simultaneously for the different sectors of the
country as follows:

Northern Viet-Nam at 8:00 a.m. (local time) on 27 July 1954

Central Viet-Nam at 8:00 a.m. (local time) on 1 August 1954

Southern Viet-Nam at 8:00 a.m. (local time) on 11 August 1954

It is agreed that Pekin mean time shall be taken as local time.

From such time as the cease-fire becomes effective in Northern
Viet-Nam, both parties undertake not to engage in any large-scale
offensive action in any part of the Indo-Chinese theatre of operations
and not to commit the air forces based on Northern Viet-Nam outside
that sector. The two parties also undertake to inform each other of
their plans for movement from one regrouping zone to another within
twenty-five (25) days of the present Agreement's entry into force.

Article 12

All the operations and movements entailed in the cessation of hostilities and regrouping must proceed in a safe and orderly fashion:

(a) Within a certain number of days after the cease-fire Agreement shall have become effective, the number to be determined on the spot by the Trung Gia Military Commission, each party shall be responsible for removing and neutralizing mines (including river- and sea-mines), booby traps, explosives and any other dangerous substances placed by it. In the event of its being impossible to complete the work of removal and neutralization in time, the party concerned shall mark the spot by placing visible signs there. All demolitions, mine fields, wire entanglements and other hazards to the free movement of the personnel of the Joint Commission and its joint groups, known to be present after the withdrawal of the military forces, shall be reported to the Joint Commission by the Commanders of the opposing forces;

(b) From the time of the cease-fire until regrouping is completed on either side of the demarcation line:

(1) The forces of either party shall be provisionally withdrawn from the provisional assembly areas assigned to the other party.

(2) When one party's forces withdraw by a route (road, rail, waterway, sea route) which passes through the territory of the other party (see Article 24), the latter party's forces must provisionally withdraw three kilometres on each side of such route, but in such a manner as to avoid interfering with the movements of the civil population.

Article 13

From the time of the cease-fire until the completion of the movements from one regrouping zone into the other, civil and military transport aircraft shall follow air-corridors between the provisional assembly areas assigned to the French Union forces north of the demarcation line on the one hand and the Laotian frontier and the regrouping zone assigned to the French Union forces on the other hand.

The position of the air-corridors, their width, the safety route for single-engined military aircraft transferred to the south and the search and rescue procedure for aircraft in distress shall be determined on the spot by the Trung Gia Military Commission.

Article 14

Political and administrative measures in the two regrouping zones, on either side of the provisional military demarcation line:

(a) Pending the general elections which will bring about the unification of Viet-Nam, the conduct of civil administration in each regrouping zone shall be in the hands of the party whose forces are to be regrouped there in virtue of the present Agreement;

(b) Any territory controlled by one party which is transferred to the other party by the regrouping plan shall continue to be administered by the former party until such date as all the troops who are to be transferred have completely left that territory so as to free the zone assigned to the party in question. From then on, such territory shall be regarded as transferred to the other party, who shall assume responsibility for it.

Steps shall be taken to ensure that there is no break in the transfer of responsibilities. For this purpose, adequate notices shall be given by the withdrawing party to the other party, which shall make the necessary arrangements, in particular by sending administrative and police detachments to prepare for the assumption of administrative responsibility. The length of such notice shall be determined by the Trung Gia Military Commission. The transfer shall be effected in successive stages for the various territorial sectors.

The transfer of the civil administration of Hanoi and Haiphong to the authorities of the Democratic Republic of Viet-Nam shall be completed within the respective time-limits laid down in Article 15 for military movements.

(c) Each party undertakes to refrain from any reprisals or discrimination against persons or organizations on account of their activities during the hostilities and to guarantee their democratic liberties.

(d) From the date of entry into force of the present Agreement until the movement of troops is completed, any civilians residing in a district controlled by one party who wish to go and live in the zone assigned to the other party shall be permitted and helped to do so by the authorities in that district.

Article 15

The disengagement of the combatants, and the withdrawals and transfers of military forces, equipment and supplies shall take place in accordance with the following principles:

(a) The withdrawals and transfers of the military forces, equipment and supplies of the two parties shall be completed within three hundred (300) days, as laid down in Article 2 of the present Agreement;

(b) Within either territory successive withdrawals shall be made by sectors, portions of sectors, or provinces. Transfers from one regrouping zone to another shall be made in successive monthly installments proportionate to the number of troops to be transferred;

(c) The two parties shall undertake to carry out all troop withdrawals and transfers in accordance with the aims of the present Agreement, shall permit no hostile act, and shall take no step whatsoever which might hamper such withdrawals and transfers. They shall assist one another as far as this is possible;

(d) The two parties shall permit no destruction or sabotage of any public property and no injury to the life and property of the civil population. They shall permit no interference in local civil administration;

(e) The Joint Commission and the International Commission shall ensure that steps are taken to safeguard the forces in the course of withdrawal and transfer:

(f) The Trung Gia Military Commission, and later the Joint Commission, shall determine by common agreement the exact procedure for the disengagement of the combatants and for troop withdrawals and transfers, on the basis of the principles mentioned above and within the framework laid down below:

1. The disengagement of the combatants, including the concentration of the armed forces of all kinds and also each party's movements into the provisional assembly areas assigned to it and the other party's provisional withdrawal from it, shall be completed within a period not exceeding fifteen (15) days after the date when the cease-fire becomes effective.

The general delineation of the provisional assembly areas is set out in the maps[1] annexed to the present Agreement.

In order to avoid any incidents, no troops shall be stationed less than 1,500 metres from the lines delimiting the provisional assembly areas.

During the period until the transfers are concluded, all the coastal islands west of the following lines shall be included in the Haiphong perimeter:

—meridian of the southern point of Kebao Island

---

[1] Not reprinted here.

—northern coast of the Ile Rousse (excluding the island), extended as far as the meridian of Campha-Mines

—meridian of Campha-Mines.

2. The withdrawals and transfers shall be effected in the following order and within the following periods (from the date of the entry into force of the present Agreement):

Forces of the French Union	*Days*
Hanoi perimeter	80
Haiduong perimeter	100
Haiphong perimeter	300

Forces of the People's Army of Viet-Nam

Ham Tan and Xuyenmec provisional assembly area	80
Central Viet-Nam provisional assembly area—first installment	80
Plaine des Joncs provisional assembly area	100
Point Camau provisional assembly area	200
Central Viet-Nam provisional assembly area—last installment	300

Chapter III—Ban on Introduction of Fresh Troops, Military Personnel, Arms and Munitions, Military Bases

Article 16

With effect from the date of entry into force of the present Agreement, the introduction into Viet-Nam of any troop reinforcements and additional military personnel is prohibited.

It is understood, however, that the rotation of units and groups of personnel, the arrival in Viet-Nam of individual personnel on a temporary duty basis and the return to Viet-Nam of individual personnel after short periods of leave or temporary duty outside Viet-Nam shall be permitted under the conditions laid down below:

(a) Rotation of units (defined in paragraph (c) of this Article) and groups of personnel shall not be permitted for French Union troops stationed north of the provisional military demarcation line laid down in Article 1 of the present Agreement, during the withdrawal period provided for in Article 2.

However, under the heading of individual personnel not more than fifty (50) men, including officers, shall during any one month be permitted to enter that part of the country north of the provisional military demarcation line on a temporary duty basis or to return there after short periods of leave or temporary duty outside Viet-Nam.

(b) "Rotation" is defined as the replacement of units or groups of personnel by other units of the same echelon or by personnel who are arriving in Viet-Nam territory to do their overseas service there;

(c) The units rotated shall never be larger than a battalion— or the corresponding echelon for air and naval forces;

(d) Rotation shall be conducted on a man-for-man basis, provided, however, that in any one quarter neither party shall introduce more than fifteen thousand five hundred (15,500) members of its armed forces into Viet-Nam under the rotation policy.

(e) Rotation units (defined in paragraph (c) of this Article) and groups of personnel, and the individual personnel mentioned in this Article, shall enter and leave Viet-Nam only through the entry points enumerated in Article 20 below.

(f) Each party shall notify the Joint Commission and the International Commission at least two days in advance of any arrivals or departures of units, groups of personnel and individual personnel in or from Viet-Nam. Reports on the arrivals or departures of units, groups of personnel and individual personnel in or from Viet-Nam shall be submitted daily to the Joint Commission and the International Commission.

All the above-mentioned notifications and reports shall indicate the places and dates of arrival or departure and the number of persons arriving or departing.

(g) The International Commission, through its Inspection Teams, shall supervise and inspect the rotation of units and groups of personnel and the arrival and departure of individual personnel as authorized above, at the points of entry enumerated in Article 20 below.

Article 17

(a) With effect from the date of entry into force of the present Agreement, the introduction into Viet-Nam of any reinforcements in the form of all types of arms, munitions and other war material, such as combat aircraft, naval craft, pieces of ordnance, jet engines and jet weapons and armoured vehicles, is prohibited.

(b) It is understood, however, that war material, arms and munitions which have been destroyed, damaged, worn out or used up after the cessation of hostilities may be replaced on the basis of piece-for-piece of the same type and with similar characteristics. Such replacements of war material, arms and munitions shall not be permitted for French Union troops stationed north of the provisional military demarcation line laid down in Article 1 of the present Agreement, during the withdrawal period provided for in Article 2.

Naval craft may perform transport operations between the regrouping zones.

(c) The war material, arms and munitions for replacement purposes provided for in paragraph (b) of this Article, shall be introduced into Viet-Nam only through the points of entry enumerated in Article 20 below. War material, arms, and munitions to be replaced shall be shipped from Viet-Nam only through the points of entry enumerated in Article 20 below;

(d) Apart from the replacements permitted within the limits laid down in paragraph (b) of this Article, the introduction of war material, arms, and munitions of all types in the form of unassembled parts for subsequent assembly is prohibited;

(e) Each party shall notify the Joint Commission and the International Commission at least two days in advance of any arrivals or departures which may take place of war material, arms and munitions of all types.

In order to justify the requests for the introduction into Viet-Nam of arms, munitions and other war material (as defined in paragraph (a) of this Article) for replacement purposes, a report concerning each incoming shipment shall be submitted to the Joint Commission and the International Commission. Such reports shall indicate the use made of the items so replaced.

(f) The International Commission, through its Inspection Teams, shall supervise and inspect the replacements permitted in the circumstances laid down in this Article, at the points of entry enumerated in Article 20 below.

Article 18

With effect from the date of entry into force of the present Agreement, the establishment of new military bases is prohibited throughout Viet-Nam territory.

Article 19

With effect from the date of entry into force of the present Agreement, no military base under the control of a foreign State may be established in the regrouping zone of either party; the two parties shall ensure that the zones assigned to them do not adhere to any military alliance and are not used for the resumption of hostilities or to further an aggressive policy.

Article 20

The points of entry into Viet-Nam for rotation personnel and replacements of material are fixed as follows:
  —Zones to the north of the provisional military demarcation line: Laokay, Langson, Tien-Yen, Haiphong, Vinh, Dong-Hoi, Muong-Sen;
  —Zones to the south of the provisional military demarcation line: Tourane, Quinhon, Nhatrang, Bangoi, Saigon, Cap St. Jacques, Tanchau.

Chapter IV—Prisoners of War and Civilian Internees

Article 21

The liberation and repatriation of all prisoners of war and civilian internees detained by each of the two parties at the coming into force of the present Agreement shall be carried out under the following conditions:

(a) All prisoners of war and civilian internees of Viet-Nam, French, and other nationalities captured since the beginning of hostilities in Viet-Nam during military operations or in any other circumstances of war and in any part of the territory of Viet-Nam shall be liberated within a period of thirty (30) days after the date when the cease-fire becomes effective in each theatre.

(b) The term "civilian internees" is understood to mean all persons who, having in any way contributed to the political and armed struggle between the two parties, have been arrested for that reason and have been kept in detention by either party during the period of hostilities.

(c) All prisoners of war and civilian internees held by either party shall be surrendered to the appropriate authorities of the other party, who shall give them all possible assistance in proceeding to their country of origin, place of habitual residence, or the zone of their choice.

Chapter V—Miscellaneous

Article 22

The Commanders of the Forces of the two parties shall ensure that persons under their respective commands who violate any of the provisions of the present Agreement are suitably punished.

Article 23

In cases in which the place of burial is known and the existence of graves has been established, the Commander of the Forces of either party shall, within a specific period after the entry into force of the Armistice Agreement, permit the graves service personnel of the other party to enter the part of Viet-Nam territory under their military control for the purpose of finding and removing the bodies of deceased military personnel of that party, including the bodies of deceased prisoners of war. The Joint Commission shall determine the procedures and the time limit for the performance of this task. The Commanders of the Forces of the two parties shall communicate to each other all information in their possession as to the place of burial of military personnel of the other party.

Article 24

The present Agreement shall apply to all the armed forces of either party. The armed forces of each party shall respect the demilitarized zone and the territory under the military control of the other party, and shall commit no act and undertake no operation against the other party and shall not engage in blockade of any kind in Viet-Nam.

For the purposes of the present Article, the word "territory" includes territorial waters and air space.

Article 25

The Commanders of the Forces of the two parties shall afford full protection and all possible assistance and co-operation to the Joint

Commission and its joint groups and to the International Commission and its inspection teams in the performance of the functions and tasks assigned to them by the present Agreement.

Article 26

The costs involved in the operations of the Joint Commission and joint groups and of the International Commission and its Inspection Teams shall be shared equally between the two parties.

Article 27

The signatories of the present Agreement and their successors in their functions shall be responsible for ensuring the observance and enforcement of the terms and provisions thereof. The Commanders of the Forces of the two parties shall, within their respective commands, take all steps and make all arrangements necessary to ensure full compliance with all the provisions of the present Agreement by all elements and military personnel under their command.

The procedures laid down in the present Agreement shall, whenever necessary, be studied by the Commanders of the two parties and, if necessary, defined more specifically by the Joint Commission.

Chapter VI—Joint Commission and International Commission for Supervision and Control in Viet-Nam

28. Responsibility for the execution of the agreement on the cessation of hostilities shall rest with the parties.

29. An International Commission shall ensure the control and supervision of this execution.

30. In order to facilitate, under the conditions shown below, the execution of provisions concerning joint actions by the two parties, a Joint Commission shall be set up in Viet-Nam.

31. The Joint Commission shall be composed of an equal number of representatives of the Commanders of the two parties.

32. The Presidents of the delegations to the Joint Commission shall hold the rank of General.

The Joint Commission shall set up joint groups the number of which shall be determined by mutual agreement between the parties. The joint groups shall be composed of an equal number of officers from both parties. Their location on the demarcation line between the re-grouping zones shall be determined by the parties whilst taking into account the powers of the Joint Commission.

33. The Joint Commission shall ensure the execution of the following provisions of the Agreement on the cessation of hostilities:

(a) A simultaneous and general cease-fire in Viet-Nam for all regular and irregular armed forces of the two parties.

(b) A re-groupment of the armed forces of the two parties.

(c) Observance of the demarcation lines between the re-grouping zones and of the demilitarized sectors.

Within the limits of its competence it shall help the parties to execute the said provisions, shall ensure liaison between them for the purpose of preparing and carrying out plans for the application of these provisions, and shall endeavor to solve such disputed questions as may arise between the parties in the course of executing these provisions.

34. An International Commission shall be set up for the control and supervision over the application of the provisions of the agreement on the cessation of hostilities in Viet-Nam. It shall be composed of representatives of the following States: Canada, India, and Poland.

It shall be presided over by the Representative of India.

35. The International Commission shall set up fixed and mobile inspection teams, composed of an equal number of officers appointed by each of the above-mentioned States. The fixed teams shall be located at the following points: Laokay, Langson, Tien-Yen, Haiphong, Vinh, Dong-Hoi, Muong-Sen, Tourane, Quinhon, Nhatrang, Bangoi, Saigon, Cap St. Jacques, Tranchau. These points of location may, at a later date, be altered at the request of the Joint Commission, or of one of the parties, or of the International Commission itself, by agreement between the International Commission and the command of the party concerned. The zones of action of the mobile teams shall be the regions bordering the land and sea frontiers of Viet-Nam, the demarcation lines between the re-grouping zones, and the demilitarized zones. Within the limits of these zones they shall have the right to move freely and shall receive from the local civil and military authorities all facilities they may require for the fulfilment of their tasks (provision of personnel, placing at their disposal documents needed for supervision, summoning witnesses necessary for holding enquiries, ensuring the security and freedom of movement of the inspection teams etc. . .). They shall have at their disposal such modern means of transport, observation, and communication as they may require. Beyond the zones of action as defined above, the mobile teams may, by

agreement with the command of the party concerned, carry out other movements within the limits of the tasks given them by the present agreement.

36. The International Commission shall be responsible for supervising the proper execution by the parties of the provisions of the agreement. For this purpose it shall fulfill the tasks of control, observation, inspection, and investigation connected with the application of the provisions of the agreement on the cessation of hostilities, and it shall in particular:

(a) Control the movement of the armed forces of the two parties, effected within the framework of the regroupment plan.

(b) Supervise the demarcation lines between the regrouping areas, and also the demilitarized zones.

(c) Control the operations of releasing prisoners of war and civilian internees.

(d) Supervise at ports and airfields as well as along all frontiers of Viet-Nam the execution of the provisions of the agreement on the cessation of hostilities, regulating the introduction into the country of armed forces, military personnel and of all kinds of arms, munitions, and war material.

37. The International Commission shall, through the medium of the inspection teams mentioned above, and as soon as possible either on its own initiative, or at the request of the Joint Commission, or of one of the parties, undertake the necessary investigations both documentary and on the ground.

38. The inspection teams shall submit to the International Commission the results of their supervision, their investigation, and their observations; furthermore, they shall draw up such special reports as they may consider necessary or as may be requested from them by the Commission. In the case of a disagreement within the teams, the conclusions of each member shall be submitted to the Commission.

39. If any one inspection team is unable to settle an incident or considers that there is a violation or a threat of a serious violation the International Commission shall be informed; the latter shall study the reports and the conclusions of the inspection teams and shall inform the parties of the measures which should be taken for the settlement of the incident, ending of the violation or removal of the threat of violation.

40. When the Joint Commission is unable to reach an agreement on the interpretation to be given to some provision or on the appraisal of a fact, the International Commission shall be informed of the dis-

puted question. Its recommendations shall be sent directly to the parties and shall be notified to the Joint Commission.

41. The recommendations of the International Commission shall be adopted by majority vote, subject to the provisions contained in Article 42. If the votes are divided, the chairman's vote shall be decisive.

The International Commission may formulate recommendations concerning amendments and additions which should be made to the provisions of the agreement on the cessation of hostilities in Viet-Nam, in order to ensure a more effective execution of that agreement. These recommendations shall be adopted unanimously.

42. When dealing with questions concerning violations, or threats of violations, which might lead to a resumption of hostilities, namely:

(a) Refusal by the armed forces of one party to effect the movements provided for in the regroupment plan;

(b) Violation by the armed forces of one of the parties of the regrouping zones, territorial waters, or air space of the other party;

the decisions of the International Commission must be unanimous.

43. If one of the parties refuses to put into effect a recommendation of the International Commission, the parties concerned or the Commission itself shall inform the members of the Geneva Conference.

If the International Commission does not reach unanimity in the cases provided for in Article 42, it shall submit a majority report and one or more minority reports to the members of the Conference.

The International Commission shall inform the members of the Conference in all cases where its activity is being hindered.

44. The International Commission shall be set up at the time of the cessation of hostilities in Indo-China in order that it should be able to fulfill the tasks provided for in Article 36.

45. The International Commission for Supervision and Control in Viet-Nam shall act in close co-operation with the International Commissions for Supervision and Control in Cambodia and Laos.

The Secretaries-General of these three Commissions shall be responsible for co-ordinating their work and for relations between them.

46. The International Commission for Supervision and Control in Viet-Nam may, after consultation with the International Commissions for Supervision and Control in Cambodia and Laos, and having regard to the development of the situation in Cambodia and Laos, progressively reduce its activities. Such a decision must be adopted unanimously.

47. All the provisions of the present Agreement, save the second sub-paragraph of Article 11, shall enter into force at 2400 hours (Geneva time) on 22 July 1954.

Done in Geneva at 2400 hours on the 20th of July 1954 in French and in Viet-Namese, both texts being equally authentic.

<table>
<tr><td>For the Commander-in-Chief of the People's Army of Viet-Nam

TA-QUANG BUU,

Vice-Minister of National Defence of the Democratic Republic of Viet-Nam</td><td>For the Commander-in-Chief of the French Union Forces in Indo-China

Brigadier-General DELTEII.</td></tr>
</table>

Appendix 1–B

Final Declaration of the Geneva Conference (July 21, 1954)

Nations taking part in the Conference: Kingdom of Cambodia, Democratic Republic of Vietnam, France, Kingdom of Laos, People's Republic of China, State of Vietnam, Union of Soviet Socialist Republics, United Kingdom (Great Britain), United States of America.

1. The Conference takes note of the agreements ending hostilities in Cambodia, Laos, and Vietnam and organizing international control and the supervision of the execution of the provisions of these agreements.

2. The Conference expresses satisfaction at the ending of hostilities in Cambodia, Laos, and Vietnam; the Conference expresses its conviction that the execution of the provisions set out in the present

[1] *Further Documents Relating to the Discussion of Indochina at the Geneva Conference* (Miscellaneous No. 20 [1954], Command Paper, 9239). London: Great Britain Parliamentary Sessional Papers, XXXI (1953-54), pp. 9-11.

declaration and in the agreements on the cessation of hostilities will permit Cambodia, Laos, and Vietnam henceforth to play their part, in full independence and sovereignty, in the peaceful community of nations.

3. The Conference takes note of the declarations made by the Governments of Cambodia and of Laos of their intention to adopt measures permitting all citizens to take their place in the national community, in particular by participating in the next general elections which, in conformity with the constitution of each of these countries, shall take place in the course of the year 1955, by secret ballot and in conditions of respect for fundamental freedoms.

4. The Conference takes note of the clauses in the agreement on the cessation of hostilities in Vietnam prohibiting the introduction into Vietnam of foreign troops and military personnel as well as of all kinds of arms and munitions. The Conference also takes note of the declarations made by the Governments of Cambodia and Laos of their resolution not to request foreign aid, whether in war material, in personnel, or in instructors except for the purpose of the effective defense of their territory and, in the case of Laos, to the extent defined by the agreements on the cessation of hostilities in Laos.

5. The Conference takes note of the clauses in the agreement on the cessation of hostilities in Vietnam to the effect that no military base under the control of a foreign State may be established in the regrouping zones of the two parties, the latter having the obligation to see that the zones allotted to them shall not constitute part of any military alliance and shall not be utilized for the resumption of hostilities or in the service of an aggressive policy. The Conference also takes note of the declarations of the Governments of Cambodia and Laos to the effect that they will not join in any agreement with other States if this agreement includes the obligation to participate in a military alliance not in conformity with the principles of the Charter of the United Nations or, in the case of Laos, with the principles of the agreement on the cessation of hostilities in Laos or, so long as their security is not threatened, the obligation to establish bases on Cambodian or Laotian territory for the military forces of foreign powers.

6. The Conference recognizes that the essential purpose of the agreement relating to Vietnam is to settle military questions with a view to ending hostilities and that the military demarcation line is provisional and should not in any way be interpreted as constituting a political or territorial boundary. The Conference expresses its con-

viction that the execution of the provisions set out in the present declaration and in the agreement on the cessation of hostilities creates the necessary basis for the achievement in the near future of a political settlement in Vietnam.

7. The Conference declares that, so far as Vietnam is concerned, the settlement of political problems, effected on the basis of respect for the principles of independence, unity, and territorial integrity, shall permit the Vietnamese people to enjoy the fundamental freedoms, guaranteed by democratic institutions established as a result of free general elections by secret ballot. In order to ensure that sufficient progress in the restoration of peace has been made, and that all the necessary conditions obtain for free expression of the national will, general elections shall be held in July, 1956, under the supervision of an international commission composed of representatives of the Member States of the International Supervisory Commission, referred to in the agreement on the cessation of hostilities. Consultations will be held on this subject between the competent representative authorities of the two zones from July 20, 1955, onward.

8. The provisions of the agreements on the cessation of hostilities intended to ensure the protection of individuals and of property must be most strictly applied and must, in particular, allow everyone in Vietnam to decide freely in which zone he wishes to live.

9. The competent representative authorities of the North and South zones of Vietnam, as well as the authorities of Laos and Cambodia, must not permit any individual or collective reprisals against persons who have collaborated in any way with one of the parties during the war, or against members of such persons' families.

10. The Conference takes note of the declaration of the Government of the French Republic to the effect that it is ready to withdraw its troops from the territory of Cambodia, Laos, and Vietnam, at the request of the Governments concerned and within periods which shall be fixed by agreement between the parties except in the cases where, by agreement between the two parties, a certain number of French troops shall remain at specified points and for a specified time.

11. The Conference takes note of the declaration of the French Government to the effect that for the settlement of all the problems connected with the re-establishment and consolidation of peace in Cambodia, Laos, and Vietnam, the French Government will proceed from the principle of respect for the independence and sovereignty, unity and territorial integrity of Cambodia, Laos, and Vietnam.

12. In their relations with Cambodia, Laos, and Vietnam, each member of the Geneva Conference undertakes to respect the sovereignty, the independence, the unity, and the territorial integrity of the above-mentioned States, and to refrain from any interference in their internal affairs.

13. The members of the Conference agree to consult one another on any question which may be referred to them by the International Supervisory Commission, in order to study such measures as may prove necessary to ensure that the agreements on the cessation of hostilities in Cambodia, Laos, and Vietnam are respected.

[This section of the Geneva Agreements was not signed by any nation, but rather agreed to by voice vote.]

Appendix 1–C

[This unilateral declaration by the United States Government sets forth its position with regard to the Geneva Accords, which it did not sign.]

Statement by the Under Secretary of State[1] at the Concluding Plenary Session of the Geneva Conference, July 21, 1954[2]

As I stated on July 18, my Government is not prepared to join in a declaration by the Conference such as is submitted. However, the United States makes this unilateral declaration of its position in these matters:

Declaration

The Government of the United States being resolved to devote its efforts to the strengthening of peace in accordance with the princi-

[1] Walter Bedell Smith.
[2] Department of State *Bulletin,* Aug. 2, 1954, pp. 162-163.

ples and purposes of the United Nations takes note of the agreements concluded at Geneva on July 20 and 21, 1954, between (a) the Franco-Laotian Command and the Command of the Peoples Army of Viet-Nam; (b) the Royal Khmer Army Command and the Command of the Peoples Army of Viet-Nam; (c) Franco-Vietnamese Command and the Command of the Peoples Army of Viet-Nam and of paragraphs 1 to 12 inclusive of the declaration presented to the Geneva Conference on July 21, 1954, declares with regard to the aforesaid agreements and paragraphs that (i) it will refrain from the threat or the use of force to disturb them, in accordance with Article 2(4) of the Charter of the United Nations dealing with the obligation of members to refrain in their international relations from the threat or use of force; and (ii) it would view any renewal of the aggression in violation of the aforesaid agreements with grave concern and as seriously threatening international peace and security.

In connection with the statement in the declaration concerning free elections in Viet-Nam my Government wishes to make clear its position which it has expressed in a declaration made in Washington on June 29, 1954, as follows:

> In the case of nations now divided against their will, we shall continue to seek to achieve unity through free elections supervised by the United Nations to insure that they are conducted fairly.

With respect to the statement made by the representative of the State of Viet-Nam, the United States reiterates its traditional position that peoples are entitled to determine their own future and that it will not join in an arrangement which would hinder this. Nothing in its declaration just made is intended to or does indicate any departure from this traditional position.

We share the hope that the agreements will permit Cambodia, Laos, and Viet-Nam to play their part, in full independence and sovereignty, in the peaceful community of nations, and will enable the peoples of that area to determine their own future.

Appendix II

Program of the National Liberation Front of South Viet-Nam[1]

[On December 20, 1960, the day of its founding, the National Liberation Front of South Viet-Nam issued a manifesto and published its ten-point program, the text of which follows:]

I. *Overthrow the camouflaged colonial regime of the American imperialists and the dictatorial power of Ngo Dinh Diem, servant of the Americans, and institute a government of national democratic union.*

The present South Vietnamese regime is a camouflaged colonial regime dominated by the Yankees, and the South Vietnamese government is a servile government, implementing faithfully all the policies of the American imperialists. Therefore, this regime must be overthrown and a government of national and democratic union put in its place composed of representatives of all social classes, of all nationalities, of the various political parties, of all religions; patriotic, eminent citizens must take over for the people the control of economic, political, social, and cultural interests and thus bring about independence, democracy, well-being, peace, neutrality, and efforts toward the peaceful unification of the country.

[1] English translation reprinted from *The Two Viet-Nams: A Political and Military Analysis* by Bernard B. Fall, published by Frederick A. Praeger, Inc., New York, 1964.

99

II. *Institute a largely liberal and democratic regime.*

1. Abolish the present constitution of the dictatorial powers of Ngo Dinh Diem, servant of the Americans. Elect a new National Assembly through universal suffrage.

2. Implement essential democratic liberties: freedom of opinion, of press, of assembly, of movement, of trade-unionism; freedom of religion without any discrimination; and the right of all patriotic organizations of whatever political tendency to carry on normal activities.

3. Proclaim a general amnesty for all political prisoners and the dissolution of concentration camps of all sorts; abolish fascist law 10/59 and all the other antidemocratic laws; authorize the return to the country of all persons persecuted by the American-Diem regime who are now refugees abroad.

4. Interdict all illegal arrests and detentions; prohibit torture; and punish all the Diem bullies who have not repented and who have committed crimes against the people.

III. *Establish an independent and sovereign economy, and improve the living conditions of the people.*

1. Suppress the monopolies imposed by the American imperialists and their servants; establish an independent and sovereign economy and finances in accordance with the national interests; confiscate to the profit of the nation the properties of the American imperialists and their servants.

2. Support the national bourgeoisie in the reconstruction and development of crafts and industry; provide active protection for national products through the suppression of production taxes and the limitation or prohibition of imports that the national economy is capable of producing; reduce customs fees on raw materials and machines.

3. Revitalize agriculture; modernize production, fishing, and cattle raising; help the farmers in putting to the plow unused land and in developing production; protect the crops and guarantee their disposal.

4. Encourage and reinforce economic relations between the city and country, the plain and the mountain regions; develop commercial exchanges with foreign countries, regardless of their political regime, on the basis of equality and mutual interests.

5. Institute a just and rational system of taxation; eliminate harassing penalties.

6. Implement the labor code: prohibition of discharges, of penalties, of ill-treatment of wage earners; improvement of the living conditions of workers and civil servants; imposition of wage scales and protective measures for young apprentices.

7. Organize social welfare: find work for jobless persons; assume

the support and protection of orphans, old people, invalids; come to the help of the victims of the Americans and Diemists; organize help for areas hit by bad crops, fires, or natural calamities.

8. Come to the help of displaced persons desiring to return to their native areas and to those who wish to remain permanently in the South; improve their working and living conditions.

9. Prohibit expulsions, spoliation, and compulsory concentration of the population; guarantee job security for the urban and rural working populations.

IV. *Reduce land rent; implement agrarian reform with the aim of providing land to the tillers.*

1. Reduce land rent; guarantee to the farmers the right to till the soil; guarantee the property right of accession to fallow lands to those who have cultivated them; guarantee property rights to those farmers who have already received land.

2. Dissolve "prosperity zones," and put an end to recruitment for the camps that are called "agricultural development centers." Allow those compatriots who already have been forced into "prosperity zones" and "agricultural development centers" to return freely to their own lands.

3. Confiscate the land owned by American imperialists and their servants, and distribute it to poor peasants without any land or with insufficient land; redistribute the communal lands on a just and rational basis.

4. By negotiation and on the basis of fair prices, repurchase for distribution to landless peasants or peasants with insufficient land those surplus lands that the owners of large estates will be made to relinquish if their domain exceeds a certain limit, to be determined in accordance with regional particularities. The farmers who benefit from such land distribution will not be compelled to make any payment or to submit to any other conditions.

V. *Develop a national and democratic culture and education.*

1. Combat all forms of culture and education enslaved to Yankee fashions; develop a culture and education that is national, progressive, and at the service of the Fatherland and people.

2. Liquidate illiteracy; increase the number of schools in the fields of general education as well as in those of technical and professional education, in advanced study as well as in other fields; adopt Vietnamese as the vernacular language; reduce the expenses of education and exempt from payment students who are without means; resume the examination system.

3. Promote science and technology and the national letters and

arts; encourage and support the intellectuals and artists so as to permit them to develop their talents in the service of national reconstruction.

4. Watch over public health; develop sports and physical education.

VI. *Create a national army devoted to the defense of the Fatherland and the people.*

1. Establish a national army devoted to the defense of the Fatherland and the people; abolish the system of American military advisers.

2. Abolish the draft system, improve the living conditions of the simple soldiers and guarantee their political rights; put an end to ill-treatment of the military; pay particular attention to the dependents of soldiers without means.

3. Reward officers and soldiers having participated in the struggle against the domination by the Americans and their servants; adopt a policy of clemency toward the former collaborators of the Americans and Diemists guilty of crimes against the people but who have finally repented and are ready to serve the people.

4. Abolish all foreign military bases established on the territory of Viet-Nam.

VII. *Guarantee equality between the various minorities and between the two sexes; protect the legitimate interests of foreign citizens established in Viet-Nam and of Vietnamese citizens residing abroad.*

1. Implement the right to autonomy of the national minorities:

Found autonomous zones in the areas with a minority population, those zones to be an integral part of the Vietnamese nation.

Guarantee equality between the various nationalities: each nationality has the right to use and develop its language and writing system, to maintain or to modify freely its mores and customs; abolish the policy of the Americans and Diemists of racial discrimination and forced assimilation.

Create conditions permitting the national minorities to reach the general level of progress of the population: development of their economy and culture; formation of cadres of minority nationalities.

2. Establish equality between the two sexes; women shall have equal rights with men from all viewpoints (political, economic, cultural, social, etc.).

3. Protect the legitimate interests of foreign citizens established in Viet-Nam.

4. Defend and take care of the interests of Vietnamese citizens residing abroad.

VIII. *Promote a foreign policy of peace and neutrality.*

1. Cancel all unequal treaties that infringe upon the sovereignty of the people and that were concluded with other countries by the servants of the Americans.

2. Establish diplomatic relations with all countries, regardless of their political regime, in accordance with the principles of peaceful coexistence adopted at the Bandung Conference.

3. Develop close solidarity with peace-loving nations and neutral countries; develop free relations with the nations of Southeast Asia, in particular with Cambodia and Laos.

4. Stay out of any military bloc; refuse any military alliance with another country.

5. Accept economic aid from any country willing to help us without attaching any conditions to such help.

IX. *Re-establish normal relations between the two zones, and prepare for the peaceful reunification of the country.*

The peaceful reunification of the country constitutes the dearest desire of all our compatriots throughout the country. The National Liberation Front of South Viet-Nam advocates the peaceful reunification by stages on the basis of negotiations and through the seeking of ways and means in conformity with the interests of the Vietnamese nation.

While awaiting this reunification, the governments of the two zones will, on the basis of negotiations, promise to banish all separatist and warmongering propaganda and not to use force to settle differences between the zones. Commercial and cultural exchanges between the two zones will be implemented; the inhabitants of the two zones will be free to move about throughout the country as their family and business interests indicate. The freedom of postal exchanges will be guaranteed.

X. *Struggle against all aggressive war; actively defend universal peace.*

1. Struggle against all aggressive war and against all forms of imperialist domination; support the national emancipation movements of the various peoples.

2. Banish all warmongering propaganda; demand general disarmament and the prohibition of nuclear weapons; and advocate the utilization of atomic energy for peaceful purposes.

3. Support all movements of struggle for peace, democracy, and social progress throughout the world; contribute actively to the defense of peace in Southeast Asia and in the world.

Appendix III

Saigon Daily News, Thursday, May 20, 1965.

Communists and Pro-Reds Outlawed Anew

SAIGON May 19 (VP)—Chief of State Phan Khac Suu on Monday proclaimed Decree Law 004/65 amending Decree Law 093-SL/CT of February 1, 1964, which outlawed Communism and pro-Communist neutralism. The Decree Law, whose contents are as follows, had been favourably voted by the National Legislative Council.

Article 1

The following actions are deemed as actions specified and punished by Decree Law 093-SL/CT of February 1, 1964:

(a) All direct or indirect actions aimed at spreading Communist policies, slogans and instructions by any individual or group of individuals influenced or controlled by the Communists.

(b) All moves which weaken the national anti-Communist effort and are harmful to the anti-Communist struggle of the people and the Armed Forces. All plots and actions under the false name of peace and neutrality according to a Communist policy and similar plots and actions are considered as belonging to the category of such moves as mentioned above.

(c) The diffusion, circulation, distribution, sale, display in public places, and the keeping of these above mentioned aims, either in printed form, drawings, photographic, or otherwise, with the same effects as stated in paragraphs *a* and *b* (Article 1).

Article 2

All associations, agencies, and organizations violating Article 1 shall be disbanded and their properties confiscated.

The Prime Minister will decide on procedures to liquidate the properties of these organizations by decrees.

Article 3

Except in cases where the "Du" No. 47 of August 21, 1956, on external security can be applied, all violations against this Decree incur a penalty of imprisonment from one to five years. Besides, the court can apply additional penalties mentioned in Art. 42 of the Modified Penal Code of Article 27 of the Penal Code (Viet Nam's ancient codes).

Article 4

The Corps Area Field Military Court, during the emergency situation, has the competence to judge all violations said in this Decree, which are caught *flagrante delicto* within the territory of the Corps Area, according to procedures contained in Decree 11-62 of May 21, 1962, on the setting up of the Field Military Court.

If not caught *flagrante delicto,* or if perpetrated in normal national situation, the perpetrations shall be tried by the military court.

Article 5

This Decree Law is promulgated according to the emergency procedure.

Appendix IV

Members of the Vietnam Working Party, AFSC

Bronson P. Clark Vice President, Guilford Instrument Laboratories, Inc., Oberlin, Ohio; member of Friends Ambulance Unit in China, 1945-46; director of China Desk, AFSC, 1947-48; director of AFSC Algerian Refugee Program, 1961-63, spending a year each in Algeria and Morocco; currently on Board of Directors of the AFSC.

Woodruff J. Emlen Investment counselor; 1944-46 administered the AFSC relief mission in North Africa and France; spent four months in Vietnam 1958 as marketing economist for Economic Co-operation Administration (now AID); one of three members of the AFSC exploratory mission to Vietnam for two months, summer 1965; currently serving on AFSC Board of Directors.

Dorothy Hutchinson International Chairman, Women's International League for Peace and Freedom; writer and lecturer on international relations; took "Journey of Friendship" around the world in 1954; member of National Speakers Bureau of United World Federalists and of the World Affairs Council of Philadelphia; author of "Toward a World Political Community" and other pamphlets and articles.

George McT. Kahin Professor of Government at Cornell University; director of Cornell's Southeast Asia Program; author of *Nationalism and Revolution in Indonesia* (1952) and *The Asian-African Confer-*

ence (1956); editor of *Governments and Politics of Southeast Asia* (1964) and *Major Governments of Asia* (1963); has contributed articles to various periodicals.

Jonathan Mirsky   Instructor, Oriental Studies Department (Chinese), University of Pennsylvania; lived and traveled in Southeast Asia 1958-61; spent summer of 1965 in South Vietnam under auspices of Inter-University Committee for Debate of Foreign Policy; on the national board of same; taught Chinese at Cambridge University, England; articles; chapters on China.

A. J. Muste   Executive Secretary of Fellowship of Reconciliation; 1940-63; Secretary Emeritus, 1963 to present; author of *Nonviolence in an Aggressive World* (1947), *Not by Might* (1947), and numerous articles; editor of *Liberation;* Associate Editor of the *Presbyterian Tribune.*

W. Allyn Rickett   Associate Professor of Chinese Studies, University of Pennsylvania; Research student and part-time lecturer at Tsinghua National University, China, 1948-50; special research student, Yenching University, China, 1950-51; author of *Prisoners of Liberation* (1957), *The Kuan-Tzu: A Repository of Early Chinese Thought* (1965), and *Legal Thought and Institutions of the People's Republic of China* (in preparation).

Clarence H. Yarrow   Secretary, International Affairs Division, AFSC; taught political science at University of Mississippi and Allegheny College; administered and taught in experimental college program for Telluride Association; Review Officer, War Labor Board, Detroit; Regional Secretary, North Central Region, AFSC; directed Around-the-World Seminar 1962.

Selected Bibliography

BARNETT, A. Doak, *Communist China and Asia: A Challenge to American Policy.* New York, Vintage V-185 (paper), 1960. 560 pp. Thorough introduction by a leading China expert.

————, *Communist China: Continuing Revolution.* Headline Series No. 153. Foreign Policy Association, May-June 1962. 60 pp. A summary of Mao's domestic and foreign policies.

————, *Communist China in Perspective.* New York, Praeger, 1962.

BROWNE, Malcom W., *The Face of War.* Indianapolis, Bobbs-Merrill, 1965. An on-the-ground report of the struggle in the South, by a Pulitzer-Prize-winning A.P. correspondent.

BURCHETT, Wilfred G., *Viet-Nam: Inside Story of the Guerrilla War.* New York, International Publishers, 1965. Written from a pro-Communist point of view, this account of warfare in South Vietnam incorporates an interesting account of the Liberation Front.

CLUBB, O. Edmund, *20th Century China.* New York, Columbia University Press, 1964. 470 pp. China's recent history, with emphasis on the impact of Communism, by a former foreign service officer who was in North China in 1949.

CLUBB, Oliver E., Jr., *The United States and the Sino-Soviet Bloc in Southeast Asia.* Washington, D.C., The Brookings Institution, 1962. A very useful account and analysis exploring aspects of American policy and its international context that less courageous and more conformist writers have avoided in their treatments.

COLE, Allan B. (ed.), *Conflict in Indo-China and International Repercussions: A Documentary History, 1945-1955*. Ithaca, N.Y., Cornell University Press, 1956. A useful collection of documents pertaining to both internal and international events.

FAIRBANK, John K., *The United States and China*. New York, Viking Press C-108 (paper), 1958 ed. 348 pp. Essential background for the present situation. A standard work by a leading Harvard specialist. An excellent introduction to modern China.

FALL, Bernard B., *Street without Joy: From the Indochina War to the War in Viet-Nam*. Harrisburg, Pa., Stackpole, 4th rev. ed., 1964. Primarily a military history of the Indochina war, 1946-54, with parallels in the new war.

———, *The Two Viet-Nams: A Political and Military History*. New York, Praeger, 5th rev. ed., 1965. A description and analysis of developments in Vietnam carrying the story through early 1964. It incorporates accounts of government and political problems in both South and North and has an excellent biography of Ho Chi Minh and others. This is one of the most useful and comprehensive coverages.

FITZGERALD, C. P., *The Chinese View of Their Place in the World*. New York, Oxford University Press, 1964. 72 pp. Traces the connection between China's past and present pretensions to world leadership.

GETTLEMAN, Marvin E. (ed.), *Vietnam: History, Documents and Opinions on a Major World Crisis*. New York, Fawcett World Library, 1965. An extremely useful compilation of sections of books, articles, and important documents that provide a good coverage of the background and conduct of the French war, the Geneva Agreements, the Diem administration, and the increasing American involvement. This is a helpful next step for those who wish to look further into questions raised in this book and the background which conditioned the American involvement. (Paperback.)

HALBERSTAM, David, *The Making of a Quagmire*. New York, Random House, 1965. An excellent account, much of it first-hand, of political and military events in South Vietnam from 1961 through 1964, with probably the best analysis available of the 1963 crisis and the fall of Diem. The writer is a correspondent for the *New York Times* who won a Pulitzer Prize for this book.

HAMMER, Ellen J., *The Struggle for Indochina*. Stanford, Stanford University Press, 1954. Probably the most comprehensive study of the French struggle to regain control over Vietnam; a basic work which contributes a great deal to the understanding of current problems.

HONEY, P. J. (ed.), *North Vietnam Today*. New York, Praeger, 1962. The nine articles in this book first appeared in the *China Quarterly*, Vols. IX and X (1962). The most useful sections are those by Philippe Devillers—on the problem of reunification; Bernard Fall— on power and pressure groups; George Ginsburgs—on local government and administration; and William Kaye—a survey of the economy and major economic problems.

KAHIN, George McT. (ed.), *Governments and Politics of Southeast Asia*. Ithaca, N.Y., Cornell University Press, 2nd ed., 1964. The 150-page section on Vietnam by Roy Jumper and Marjorie Weiner Normand provides brief but comprehensive coverage of the modern political development of both North and South Vietnam with sections on historical background, contemporary setting, political processes, and major problems. There are also sections on Cambodia and Laos by Roger Smith that incorporate material relevant to some of the problems discussed in this book.

KUO PING-CHIA, *China New Age and New Outlook*. Penguin Books (S-179), 1960. A stimulating and challenging analysis of the Chinese revolution and of the first decade of the Communist regime by a well-known Chinese historian, now at Southern Illinois University.

LANCASTER, Donald, *The Emancipation of French Indochina*. London, Oxford University Press, 1961. A political history of the achievement of independence, largely devoted to Vietnam. A comprehensive and useful political history, one of the best in English, by a former member of the British diplomatic establishment.

LI, CHOH-MING (ed.), *Industrial Development in Communist China*. A special issue (No. 17, 1964) of the periodical *China Quarterly* (London), which has also been reprinted in book form.

MECKLIN, John, *Mission in Torment*. New York, Doubleday, 1965. A revealing inside report by a former high official of the United States Information Agency in Saigon concerning errors in American policy and its conduct.

MURTI, B. S. N., *Vietnam Divided*. New York, Asia Publishing House, 1964. The fullest account, other than the actual records, of the findings of the International Control Commission, especially useful for the period 1954-57, during which the author served as Deputy Secretary-General and Public Relations Officer of the I.C.C.

OSBORNE, Milton E., *Strategic Hamlets in South Viet-Nam: A Survey and a Comparison.* Data Paper No. 55, Southeast Asia Program, Cornell University, 1965. The fullest published account: it provides a searching assessment of this unsuccessful program and points to the very different circumstances attending the earlier resettlement program in Malaya.

RASKIN, Marcus G., and FALL, Bernard B. (eds.), *The Viet-Nam Reader.* New York, Vintage Books, 1965. An extremely useful and comprehensive compendium of various articles and documents relating to the background and development of the American involvement in Vietnam; it should be one of the first things referred to by anyone wishing to develop a fuller understanding of the problems discussed in this book. (Available in paperback.)

ROBEQUAIN, Charles, *The Economic Development of French Indo-China.* London, Oxford University Press, 1944. The major survey of the French colonial economy. First published in French in 1939; it includes a supplement, "Recent Developments in Indo-China, 1939-1943" by John Andrus and Katrine R. C. Greene.

SCIGLIANO, Robert, *South Vietnam: Nation under Stress.* Boston, Houghton Mifflin Co., 1963. Probably the most comprehensive and objective account of the South Vietnamese regime, covering the period until just before the fall of Diem. (Available in paperback.)

SNOW, Edgar, *The Other Side of the River: Red China Today.* New York, Random House, 1961. 810 pp. A long, sympathetic account of the Communist regime by almost the only U.S. journalist with recent access to Mao and Chou. Snow interviewed top Communist leaders after the Long March and more recently in Peking.

TANHAM, George K., *Communist Revolutionary Warfare: The Vietminh in Indochina.* New York, Praeger, 1961. A good analysis of the organization, operations, and tactics of the Viet Minh in their successful struggle against the French.

ZAGORIA, Donald S., *The Sino-Soviet Conflict, 1956-1961.* Princeton, Princeton University Press, 1962. Detailed study of how the Sino-Soviet rift came about.

BOOKS IN FRENCH

There are a few extremely important books in French which should be consulted by those who have competence in that language.

CHAFFARD, Georges, *Indochine dix ans à indépendance*. Paris, Calman Levy, 1964. An informative account by a correspondent of *Le Monde* who had undertaken considerable travel in Vietnam between 1949 and 1963.

DEVILLERS, Philippe, *Histoire du Viet-Nam de 1940 à 1952*. Paris, Editions du Seuil, 1952. A comprehensive and scholarly study which is especially enlightening for the 1945-49 period. Probably the soundest and most comprehensive study of this period in any language; by a well-established French scholar who had direct experience in Vietnam.

LACOUTURE, Jean, and DEVILLERS, Philippe, *La fin d'une guerre: Indochine 1954*. Paris, Editions du Seuil, 1960. A detailed account of events in Vietnam during the period 1945-54, which culminated in the defeat of France at Dienbienphu and the partition of Vietnam at the Geneva Conference.

LACOUTURE, Jean, *Le Viet-Nam entre deux Paix*. Paris, Editions du Seuil, 1965. An excellent and well-informed account of the decade since Geneva by a first-rate French journalist (to be published in English by Random House, 1966).

MUS, Paul, *Viet-Nam: Sociologie d'une guerre*. Paris, Editions du Seuil, 1952. An informative treatment of sociological and cultural aspects of the French-Vietnamese conflict.